# Needlepoint for the Whole Family

*Books By Nina Mortellito*

RIGHT OR LEFT IT'S NEEDLEPOINT

THE SMALL KITCHEN COOKBOOK

# NEEDLEPOINT
## for the
# WHOLE FAMILY

### Nina Mortellito

WALKER AND COMPANY · NEW YORK

Copyright © 1973 by Nina Mortellito

All rights reserved.
No part of this book may be reproduced or transmitted in any form
or by any means, electronic or mechanical, including photocopying,
recording, or by any information storage and retrieval system,
without permission in writing from the Publisher.

First published in the United States of America in 1973
by the Walker Publishing Company, Inc.

Published simultaneously in Canada by Fitzhenry & Whiteside, Limited, Toronto.

ISBN: 0-8027-0425-5

Library of Congress Catalog Card Number: 72-96496

Printed in the United States of America.

Designed by Jack Jaget

10 9 8 7 6 5 4 3 2

*In loving memory of my grandfather*

# ACKNOWLEDGMENTS

Between the contract to write a book and the actual writing of the manuscript lies a rough ocean for an amateur—it's sink or swim. That responsibility lies with a good copy editor—I had the best, Bea Losito. Thanks to her talents as an editor and hours of hard work, this book went to press. My heartfelt thanks.

Much gratitude to Kathleen Beakely, who typed this book in record time, created order from chaos and gave us a beautiful manuscript to work from.

Also, many thanks to my long-suffering and infinitely patient friends who allowed me to use them as sounding-boards.

I am particularly grateful to the following people who allowed me to show their beautiful needlepoint in this book:

Harriet Kravitz: Jacket photograph of tiger family

Andrée Devendorf: Giraffe tennis racket cover, Christmas stockings

Carol Devendorf: Jaguar cub address book, coasters, pin cushion, doorstop, Christmas tree decorations, mirror, Christmas stockings

Gertrude Golding: Rectangular stitchery pillow

Nena Goodman: Butterfly rug, safari animal head pillows

Adrienne Gordon: Zinnia pillow

Dottie Gossler: Leopard and cubs rug

Louise Hendrix: "Tucon Pete" stitchery pillow

Rosemary Keating: Handbuilt and decorated chair with stitchery seat

Herb Mesick: Initial and geometric pillow (two sides)

Blanche Shapiro: Owl, tiger cub, and kitten pillows, poppy picture frame

Elizabeth Simmons: Alligator rug
Joyce Stearns: Hippopotamus, lion cub, and square stitchery pillows
Roland Stearns: Giraffe telephone book cover
Beth Walker: Zebra chair, leopard cub footstool


*Photographs by Dennis Barna, Don Jackson and Bonne Stearns*

# Contents

# Preface

I N selling a variety of needlepoint books at my shop, I have become increasingly aware of both their strengths and weaknesses. A general needlepoint book must provide clear, concise instructions in the basic methods and materials used in the craft. It should suggest a variety of projects that anyone can do, and map them out in detail from beginning to end. This is particularly important in areas throughout the country where facilities and materials are not widely available. Finally, the book should present new inspirations and goals, and the challenge of more advanced stitches to people who have already started needlepointing.

I made up my mind to write my own book to answer in print the questions that are answered every day in my shop. Questions such as: where did needlepoint orginate? why has it gained such popularity? why are most instructions so difficult to follow? why does a left-hander have to learn from right-handed diagrams? why is the technique of shading still a mystery? what do terms like warp and woof mean? and how do you put all the pieces of information together and come up with a completed piece of needlepoint?

With all the why's, where's and how's it appears that, despite all the books on needlepoint presently available, there is still a lingering mysticism about needlepoint techniques. Therefore the aim of this book is to dispel that mysticism and replace it with working knowledge.

Since I am involved not only in the design and production of needlepoint, but also in close association with the people who purchase and sew my designs, it seems appropriate to share the difficulties as well as the accomplishments, that we and our dedicated needlepointers have experienced, with other needlepointers.

Children enjoy needlepoint just as much as adults do, and it is no longer considered strictly a "woman's hobby" (many men have evinced great interest and aptitude in doing it). So you will now find entire families engaged in this fascinating and creative activity. Whether Mom, Dad, Sister or Brother chooses to do an individual project, or they want to join together in sewing a group project, I have included appropriate instructions and designs. It is because of all of you, and for all of you, that this book is written.

# Introduction

I HAVE always had a deep love for animals, both domestic and wild. My love grew naturally in a home filled with household pets (birds, fish, cats, dogs, turtles, lizards, and even a goat!). My mother is a nationally known sculptor, famous for her carvings of animals, and when I was very young, she would take me to the zoo to sketch. On special days, I was allowed to model in clay at her studio—my subject matter was always animals.

My first exposure to needlepoint was an impulse purchase, when I was fourteen, of a pillow with a lily pattern already stitched in the center—my project was to fill in the background. It seemed deceptively easy; until I had coped with turning corners, that is. Having stitched the canvas too tightly and pulled it into the most unrecognizable shape, I set about blocking it, believing that if a little water is good for blocking, lots would be even better! I applied this same theory to nailing the canvas to the board. There was a nail every quarter inch. I'm afraid that piece of needlepoint didn't have much of a chance. Three days later, it was dry, and though not quite square, it was passable. The mounting was not, but it was a beginning.

When I was nineteen, my friend, Lukie Reilly (who later became my partner) and I designed twenty pieces of needlepoint for my grandmother's antique shop in the Bahamas. We then duplicated these designs, and, on a lark, showed them to Alice Maynard, who bought all of them. We also freelanced for Maynard while working at other fulltime jobs with which we were not particularly happy, and in 1958, we opened our own business, calling it "Sorelle," (Sisters) which was operated out of my mother's house. Our initial capital was $180 of which $60 was spent on printing our business announcements! We sent out the announcements, and then sat back and waited for our first customer.

Although we did fairly well that first year, we were too young and naive to be in business, and in 1959 we decided to shut down. Lukie went off to California to live, and I went to work at the Carstairs Gallery as a receptionist, while attending the American Art School. Lukie had done all the drawing for our business and I had merely filled in colors, so I decided I needed the knowhow of drawing techniques. It was essential to learn all the aspects of drawing, perspective, and repeat design. My goal now was to go to Europe to live, but for that I needed money, and since I knew needlepoint, I decided that would pay my way. I was now using my own name, Nina Mortellito, and I did earn enough to be able to go to Paris, where I lived for two and a half years, selling needlepoint designs to *Elle* magazine whenever I needed pocket money. I studied art and was going to become a sculptor. Upon my return to the United States I studied sculpture with my mother, Jane Wasey, and also did some book illustrations, which eventually led to the *Small Kitchen Cookbook* published by Walker and written and illustrated by me.

From 1964-1966 I sculpted, and did pen and ink drawings, always of animals. I exhibited them all over the Northeast, and although I was commissioned to sculpt and had sold some pieces, the income was erratic. I once again fell back on needlepoint as a means of earning my livelihood, and in 1966 I found myself back in the needlepoint world.

It was just beginning to take on life, and as it was impossible for me to give up my animal drawings, I decided to bring fine art to needlepoint and depict the animals I love so much. The shops were not convinced this would be a popular needlepoint theme, but public response brought me more work than I could handle. Gradually I began training people to copy my designs for me, and the business grew too big for my studio apartment, forcing me to move into a larger one. Within a year, when I had to move my art table into the kitchen, I knew we would have to have a proper studio. We were wholesaling all over the country by then. My friend, Lukie, rejoined me and we found a vacant doctor's office on the Upper East Side, where we set up our business.

My sister, Jebba, had also started a needlepoint business of her own on the West Coast. She rented part of our quarters for her business, having her kits assembled for the stores she supplied in the East.

Our business continued to grow, and in 1970, we plunged into the retail end incorporated as Nina Needlepoint, moving to our present address at 860 Madison Avenue.

If someone were to ask me if I had ever thought this would happen, the answer would have to be "no"—there we were, running a small business in a studio apartment, and, four years later, we had a Madison Avenue shop, with twenty people working for us!

Needlepoint brings out the best and worst in people—success or failure, it is never dull, and it would be impossible to be in the needlepoint business for any length of time without encountering funny, sad and frustrating experiences.

For instance, needlepoint has become such big business that it is constantly being stolen. Unsewn designs with the yarn are fenced in New Jersey, and pieces in progress are lifted from hotel rooms, or out of satchels while customers are shopping. One lady purchasing some dog food at a supermarket, set her Gucci tote bag containing a partially sewn vest, down beside her. When she turned around, the Gucci bag was still there—but the needlepoint was gone! Another woman carefully locked her jewels up in the hotel safe, but left her needlepoint on the bed in her room. When she returned, her needlepoint was gone. "Next time," she said, "I'm going to have my needlepoint locked up in the safe." If this should happen (which I doubt), the hotels are sure going to have to expand their vault areas!

One terrible day, a gentleman came by to pick up a beautiful needlepoint chair for one of our customers. He asked for it by name, signed for it, and later was seen trying to sell it on the street. He had offered it to a woman for twenty dollars. That week, the lady to whom he had offered it, was telling her story to friends during a bridge game, remarking, "Sue, it looked just like the one you did . . . " and indeed it was! We replaced it for her, but somewhere someone is sitting on a beautiful sandpiper director's chair that was bought off the street.

Then there was the lady who couldn't understand why the lining had shrunk on her vest after one wearing and a little spot cleaning—in the washing machine! Needlepoint and washing machines were not made for each other.

Often, a strong possessive attachment is formed for the design being sewn. To lose it or have it ruined is a fate worse than death, or so it would seem. There was a woman who was stitching while aboard her yacht; as it pulled out of the harbor, her canvas fell overboard. The alarm went out. All engines dead slow, a dinghy with two men aboard was lowered to retrieve it. (By the way, needlepoint floats quite well.) Safely back on board, it was laid out to dry—to no avail, for the piece was ruined by the salt water, and the sun didn't help.

Sewing errors are often blamed on the shop where they are purchased. No store or saleswoman is infallible, but it is a sure bet that they will not intentionally set themselves up for trouble. One such mistake was sewn round and round; the customer having worked from the outside in, found it extremely difficult to fit the stitches into the middle, and the canvas with the stitches pulling in four different directions was impossible to block. Another woman who had laboriously folded under the edges of her canvas and sewed through three layers without missing a stitch, wanted her piece blocked, "but please don't use any nails," said she. An impossible request, but after all "they" had told her that that was the way to do it.

Custom orders involve me in curious situations. Since I do a great many dog portraits, I am constantly faced with humorous moments. Dogs are more than welcome at our shop, and they enjoy visiting, because they know they will always be patted, and get a biscuit. Customers, knowing this, love to bring them in. Eventually their pets will be depicted on canvas and immortalized in needlepoint. Sometimes the client lives out of town, so photographs are sent in to work from. It was with great surprise and bewilderment that, upon opening my mail one morning, I found three beautiful snapshots of a dog, and a very large clump of its hair, so that I could match the coloring exactly. The idea was fine, and it did help, but it was the quantity of hair that threw me. Some dog was walking around with a large bald spot, all for the sake of needlepoint!

My favorite incident occurred when a gentleman appeared with a small, longhaired dachshund. It was vital that I see the dog's coloring, head shape and lovable eyes. Upon asking the gentleman what measurement the canvas should be, he replied, "a small coin purse." He then went on to explain that he wanted the dog depicted in an ark-type boat with a palm tree. With all of that, the dog's head was reduced to the size of a thumbnail. Working on #18 canvas, the eyes were one stitch each, and only the owner could know that the dog in the boat was his!

Needlepoint is work, and it should be happy work, considering the number of hours spent on it. Whether a canvas is stitched as a gift or for personal pleasure, it will be around for a few hundred years if properly cared for. An interesting thought is what people will think about this art form a hundred years from now. It should tell them a fair amount about us, for it marks an era of handwork, bright colors, fashion, home decorating, and a plethora of productivity. With all the needlepoint that will have been done, they might say "They were keeping the family in stitches."

Needlepoint is a highly competitive business and we are known for our technical ability in producing good designs. I have seen a few good copies, but the majority are badly executed and cause great confusion to our clientele. I have always felt strongly that any design which goes out to a customer, whether it is retail or wholesale, must be of the best quality. All of our art work is done on our premises to insure the closest possible quality control, and I believe this is one of the major factors in our success.

One of the delights of my needlepoint career has been the combination of my life-long passion for animals, with my work. My trips to Africa have influenced me tremendously, because watching animals in their wild and natural habitats not only restores a sense of proportion to my life, but instills a lasting inspiration in me to try to bring others a sense of the beauty of what I have seen, and a new dimension to needlepoint.

# Needlepoint for the Whole Family

# Part I
# BASIC TECHNIQUE

# Chapter 1

# Stitches in Time

NEEDLES were first made ten thousand years ago, out of stone, fishbone, iron or bronze. Some lacked eyes, and so were like an awl to punch holes through which thongs of leather, or plant fibers could be drawn. Others had eyes for carrying the thread at the point (similar to the modern shoemaker's awl). Still others had the eyes halfway between the point and the head. In the sixth century B.C., needles with the eye at the head were used in China for embroidery work. However, documenting the history of a needle is much simpler than tracing the origin of needlepoint, as you will learn.

The difficulty in tracing the history of needlework is due in part to the terminology, (see Photographs 1-3). For example, the famous eleventh century Bayeux tapestry depicting the Battle of Hastings in 1066 is *not* tapestry. It is a piece of embroidery, awesome in its two hundred thirty-one foot length. The first hint of the existence of needlepoint as a separate entity appears in the early 1500s with the mention of the term "Tent Stitch" (one of the few words that has never changed in its use). The word "needlepoint," as we know it, was not used until the end of the seventeenth century. The term "woven linen cloth" was used during the sixteenth and seventeenth centuries to describe canvas. It was not until 1830, when the first proper looms were built, that the word "canvas" was used, and a mass produced double meshed canvas became readily available.

There is little doubt that the Italian craftsmen dominated the embroidery world in the early 1600s. They traveled to China, Persia, and the Near East to obtain silk and metallic threads and materials. Beautiful lengths of silk woven in these distant countries bore distinctive designs that influenced the Europeans.

The English often traded directly with Europe for these materials, and therefore Europe and England were both exposed to the same motifs that so greatly influenced their embroidery work. Much like today, there were periods when importing was limit-

Photograph 1. Tapestry

Photograph 2. Crewel

Photograph 3. Needlepoint

ed by the government, or trade routes were severed due to political situations. Trade would then commence with other countries, and new elements of design and techniques were brought back to Europe. A good example of this influence from distant lands is noted when the English began trade with India in 1613. Englishmen brought home fabrics bearing leaf patterns in an infinity of background variations. The designs were a natural for needlepoint. Many of the backgrounds in needlepoint were filled in using these leaf motifs, and this period is referred to as the Jacobean period of needlepoint.

The sixteenth, seventeenth, and early eighteenth centuries saw needlepoint flourish, particularly in England, France, and Italy. Henry VIII and Elizabeth I were enthusiastic about this art form, and encouraged their artisans to produce lavish wall hangings, cushions, bookcovers, gloves, shoes, purses, and pictures. Wall hangings and cushions were as functional as they were decorative; in the drafty castles, wall hangings gave warmth and some privacy. Furniture carved from hard woods was made more comfortable with cushions. Elaborate clothing was adorned with bits of needlepoint appliqued on to the clothing in small sections. Religious scenes and battles were intricately stitched, with some pieces of needlepoint containing four hundred stitches per square inch!

The Marquise de Maintenon, Louis XIV's secret and last wife, established a school for the poor girls of the nobility at St. Cyr in France. There, in 1686, needlepoint infiltrated the school curriculum. After Louis' death, Mme. Maintenon established herself at the school, and there she remained teaching until her death. There are several magnificent needlepoint wall hangings still to be seen hanging in Versailles, stitched by her pupils.

Embroidery pattern books date back to 1631, when they were published in England and France. They offered colored diagrams and a variety of stitches.

In the late seventeenth century, Italy introduced the Florentine, or Flame Stitch, commonly referred to as Bargello. There was an urge to speed work up—much as Bargello has been used for speed today, it was used for the same purpose in the 1700s.

For three hundred years, needlepoint was detailed and laboriously stitched. The majority of work had been done by artisans, professionals in embroidery who traveled from country to country as they were hired, sometimes staying only long enough to complete a needlepoint commission. One craftsman might work in several different countries, for fairly short periods of time, so it is difficult today to distinguish the country or origin of many of the older pieces of needlepoint.

More and more needlepoint was being done by laymen, and these non-professionals demanded canvas that took larger stitches. Germany led the way with the production of a larger, even-meshed canvas. Berlin Wool Work came into fashion, with its brilliant worsteds. It was a bold pictorial style of needlepoint. Fourteen thousand painted charts of different designs were published, making Berlin Wool Work readily available to everyone. The style quickly spread through Europe and on to America.

From the intricate and delicate, to the simple and bold, needlepoint had established itself as a beautiful and lasting creative art form, adaptable in its uses and destined to endure the wear and tear of time. However, there was one serious drawback: it required leisure hours. With the turn of the twentieth century, needlepoint became a dormant activity. People were caught up in the hustle and bustle of everyday activities. When the First World War came, women devoted their free hours to rolling bandages and knitting for their men overseas. Then came the Depression, and needlepoint was forgotten, as it could hardly be considered an essential when money was so tight. On the heels of the Depression, the Second World War began, and, once again, women threw themselves into handwork for their men overseas, or took jobs that normally would have been filled by men.

And so it was that needlepoint was all but forgotten for about fifty years. Everyone had become accustomed to knitting, due to necessity. Children born during this period learned to knit early in their lives, and later, as teenagers, were knitting everything from cabled sweaters to winter caps with pompoms, to argyle socks. Knitting yarn was available in new, tantalizing colors. Professional knitters were capable of making dresses, coats, skirts, and jackets which were cheaper and more chic than those available in the department stores, but the average knitter, unable to follow the complicated instructions for clothing, began to look around for a different form of handwork.

Certainly leisure hours were becoming greater with prosperity and the increasing availability of frozen foods, dishwashers and all the handy helpers freeing women from household drudgery. Women who had grown accustomed to going out to work during the War, continued their jobs. They were earning good money, and it was theirs to spend. Why not on needlepoint?

Although needlepoint began to experience a revival of interest, it was still being done slowly, laboriously and with painstaking detail, requiring large amounts of time. This meant that the craft remained rather limited in its appeal, technique, and design. However, during the past several years, innovative techniques and designs have broadened and spectacularly increased its popularity.

Needlepoint did not become a rage overnight. It was the demand of the general public which forced life back into it. For, during the dormant years, very few new designs were created. There were a myriad of presewn floral and fruit patterns on brown penelope canvas. The only decisions left to the purchasers were which fruit or flower pattern to choose, and what color to use for the background. Hardly inspiring or stimulating, but it was a switch from knitting. The few handpainted designs available were eagerly snatched up. People wanted needlepoint. Slowly the resurgence began. The needlework stores were still set in their ways, and took refuge in the safety of tried and true, old-fashioned designs. Artists were sorely needed to contribute their talents and fresh ideas to needlepoint. Confined by limited yarn colors, it was to become an uphill battle. I know all this for a fact, as I became involved in needlepoint designing at this time (about fifteen years ago). My partner, Lukie Reilly, and I soon discovered the voracious appetite of the public for new designs. Paternayan Bros., the yarn firm we have dealt with from the beginning, expanded their range of Persian yarn colors, freeing needlepoint from the dusty rose syndrome.

Home decorating was becoming a new and wonderful pastime. It was also the commencement of the "do it yourself" era with all the necessary equipment for almost any project purchasable at a reasonable price. Needlepoint was a natural for this upsurge in redecorating. It had color, design, creativity, and, above all, it was an art form. Every home decorating magazine featured it, and soon pictures and articles were appearing in almost every publication, picturing the "beautiful people" doing it. It was quickly established as the "in" thing to be seen doing. An increasing selection of designs was available, from simple and chic, to intricate and exciting . . . and needlepoint was there for everyone.

The limitless uses of design, color, and texture challenged needlepointers' creativity. They, in turn, spurred the designers on to draw and paint canvases at a staggering rate. Needlepoint, no longer limited to chairs, footstools, and rugs, now covered picture frames, doorbricks, valances, stereo speakers, walls, screens, headboards, pillows of every size and shape, card table covers, luggage racks, cigarette, card, and jewelry boxes, telephone and address books, coasters, flyswatters, breakfast and cocktail trays, lamps, and ice buckets. All were covered and smothered in thousands of colorful stitches. Not confined to the home, needlepoint walked out of the house in such forms as vests, belts, cummerbunds, suspenders, pocketbooks, tennis, squash, and paddle racket covers, golf club covers, pocket patches, eyeglass cases, and shoes.

With the variations in sizes and shapes, design became of prime importance. It had turned needlepoint into one of the fastest growing competitive businesses in the United States. Europe was left behind in an art that had originally been created there. It was a stitcher's delight and a designer's nightmare. Shops were opening up every day all over the country, bringing people what they demanded . . . *needlepoint.* The public was now able to pick and choose, as there was an abundance of designs to select from.

About ten years ago, commercial needlepoint kits began to come into their own. They contain stamped, silkscreened, heat transferred, or mass produced, half screened, half handpainted, designs. The design is done simply in distinct flat colors on an inexpensive cotton canvas on either mono or penelope canvas. The most popular canvas for kits has ten stitches to the inch. Kits come with basic instructions, needle, and sufficient yarn to complete each color in the design, (see Photograph 4).

Photograph 4. Needlepoint kit on penelope canvas.

For those who prefer the flexibility and exclusivity of a handpainted design, there are an increasing number of professionals available who will execute designs varying in style and degree of difficulty, from the simplest, in limited colors, to the most complicated, with unlimited colors and shading. Each design is drawn on the canvas with waterproof ink, and handpainted in oils or acrylics. The canvas is of the highest quality, imported from Europe, ranging from ten stitches to the inch to eighteen stitches to the inch, allowing the most intricate designs to be sewn distinctly, (see Photograph 5). There is a different size needle for each mesh (see Illustrated Dictionary). At the time of purchase, the wools are "pulled" individually, allowing the purchaser to change color combinations and select an appropriate background color. Should there be any problems or assistance needed, the courtesy of a knowledgeable helping hand goes with your purchase. Any extra yarn needed, should there be a shortage, will be given free of charge, and is readily available. It is therefore easily understandable why designs of this caliber, sold in this manner, are much more costly than kit designs.

Specialized or personalized designs can be ordered and professionally executed at any good needlepoint shop. Most shops have a distinctive style and it soon becomes easy to distinguish one designer's work from another. With all the hours spent creating a canvas on the part of designers and painters, however, it is the person who does the stitching who gains the lasting satisfaction from it; it is an artistic achievement, and a labor of love.

Photograph 5. Handpainted design on mono canvas with Persian yarn.

# Chapter 2

# It's More Than Just a Stitch

LET ME begin by saying that everyone has set ideas on how to teach needlepoint and how to diagram stitches. Quite naturally, we each feel our way is better than someone else's. We have been using this method to teach these stitches for several years, and from the high percentage of successes, feel safe in passing it on to you. If it is any encouragement, you are not the first to try it. As you follow the numbered diagrams, you will notice that *when no new number is given to a hole, it is because you are going back into a hole you have used before.*

Threading the needle can be more difficult for the beginner than learning the basic stitch. Everyone can eventually do it, though I have known some people to take an hour and a half to get the hang of it. So, if you think this is going to present a problem, don't be disturbed. Keep your temper, keep laughing, and keep trying—you can do it, and here's how.

### THREADING THE NEEDLE

| Left-Handed | Figure 1 | Right-Handed |
|:---:|:---:|:---:|

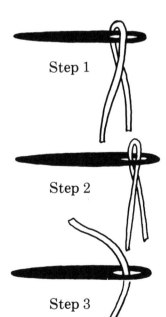

Loop the wool over the eye of the needle
Pinch the wool tightly against the needle
*Don't let go*

Slip the needle out—keeping the wool
   tightly pinched
Ease the tightly pinched wool through
   the eye of the needle
(A slight sawing motion with the
   needle helps)

Pull one piece of the wool completely
   through the eye of the needle

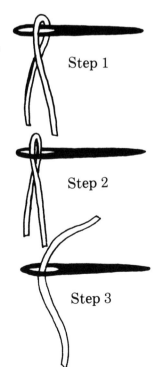

Step 1

Step 2

Step 3

27

I have found that the most difficult part of this maneuver comes when coaxing the wool through the eye of the needle. Most people release the wool too early. You must keep pinching it until it is through the needle's eye.

There are three basic stitches in needlepoint. They are: the Half Cross, the Continental or Tent, and the Basketweave. I have very strong opinions about these three stitches. The Basketweave takes precedence over the other two, as it is durable, even, and puts the least amount of strain on the canvas. It also has one overwhelming advantage: worked on the diagonal, it allows you to hold the canvas right side up at all times so you can see where you are going. This is particularly important when shading a design. This stitch takes its name from the pattern it forms on the reverse side, a woven basket affect. It is essential to keep the back and forth rhythm on the diagonal rows, as it is this unbroken pattern that forms the interweaving. Run two rows in the same direction and it will form a ridge in front, even though the stitches look correct. This happens because those two rows did not interlock. To easily avoid this, *always stop in the middle of a row,* then you will always know which direction you are heading in. If this should happen, it might be of consolation to you to know that it also happens to the experts.

The Continental Stitch is perfect for the small child. It is difficult for children to grasp the concept of sewing on the diagonal. They are quick to catch on to the Continental, as you go straight across a row, turn the canvas around so that it is upside down, and go straight back across that row, etc. In teaching a child, it is helpful to write "Top" and "Bottom" on their canvas. Don't be alarmed when the canvas goes out of shape. This stitch pulls at the canvas, but it can be stretched back into shape when it is blocked.

To me, the Half Cross has always been a useless stitch. The only thing in its favor is that, if you are saving on yarn, this stitch uses the least of all, and because it does, it leaves you with a flimsy piece of needlepoint. So, even if I am offending those who enjoy the Half Cross, forgive me, but it is one stitch I refuse to teach.

To get started, you need a piece of canvas—#10 mono is perfect. A small square, 6″ x 6″, is ideal. Put masking tape around the edges to keep it from fraying and snagging the yarn. With a #3 pencil, mark out a square, keeping your lines in the valleys (see Figure 2, Steps 1, 2 and 3). Now take a #18 needle and thread it with one strand of yarn.

Figure 2

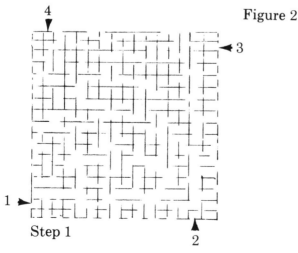

Step 1

Start each strip of tape at arrow marks 1,2,3,4

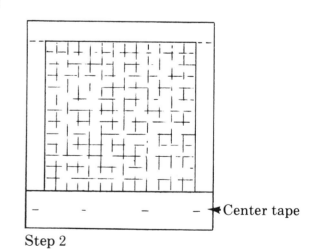

Step 2

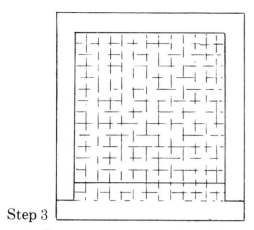

Step 3

Turn canvas over and seal tape down

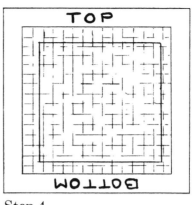

Step 4

For those ten years and younger, we'll begin with the Continental.

Hold the canvas in your *right hand if you are left-handed*, and *in your left hand if you are right-handed*, with the marking "Top" at the top (see Step 4).

Starting in the upper corner, poke your needle up from the back through the hole marked number 1, one in from your pencil mark in the top corner (see Diagram 1).

## CONTINENTAL STITCH

### FIRST ROW

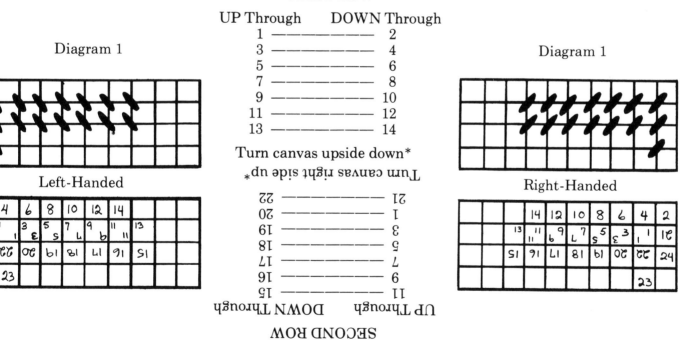

| UP Through | DOWN Through |
|:---:|:---:|
| 1 ———————— | 2 |
| 3 ———————— | 4 |
| 5 ———————— | 6 |
| 7 ———————— | 8 |
| 9 ———————— | 10 |
| 11 ———————— | 12 |
| 13 ———————— | 14 |

Turn canvas upside down*

*Turn canvas right side up*

| DOWN Through | UP Through |
|:---:|:---:|
| 22 ———————— | 21 |
| 20 ———————— | 1 |
| 19 ———————— | 3 |
| 18 ———————— | 5 |
| 17 ———————— | 7 |
| 16 ———————— | 9 |
| 15 ———————— | 11 |

SECOND ROW

### THIRD ROW

| UP Through | DOWN Through |
|:---:|:---:|
| 23 ———————— | 24 |

* Always turn the book upside down or right side up when turning the canvas

Diagram 1

Left-Handed

| 4 | 6 | 8 | 10 | 12 | 14 | | | | |
|---|---|---|---|---|---|---|---|---|---|
| 1 | 3 | 5 | 7 | 9 | 11 | 13 | | | |
| | | | | | | | | | |
| 22 | 20 | 18 | 16 | 14 | 12 | | | | |
| 23 | | | | | | | | | |

Diagram 1

Right-Handed

| | | 14 | 12 | 10 | 8 | 6 | 4 | 2 | |
|---|---|---|---|---|---|---|---|---|---|
| | | 13 | 11 | 9 | 7 | 5 | 3 | 1 | 21 |
| | | 15 | 16 | 17 | 18 | 19 | 20 | 22 | 24 |
| | | | | | | | | 23 | |

*Gently* pull the yarn through until one inch remains dangling on the reverse side. Hold this dangling end against the back of the canvas with your index finger. This loose end will be caught and held down by your next stitches. *Knots are never used* on the back of a canvas either to begin or end a piece of yarn, as they form lumps. Now, following the numbered instructions, poke your needle down through the hole marked 2 and you have completed your first needlepoint stitch. You're on your way! When you have used up all but three inches of yarn, poke your needle through to the back (completing a stitch), turn your canvas over, and slip your needle through six stitches on the back. Pull the yarn through, and snip off the tail.

For those over ten years of age, here is the Basketweave Stitch. You need a 6″ x 6″ piece of #10 mono canvas, with masking tape around the edges, an outline of a square penciled in and a threaded #18 needle. It is helpful to mark "Top" at the top of the square. As the canvas is never turned around, it is not necessary to add any other markings.

With the marking "Top" at the top, hold the canvas in your *right hand if you are left-handed*, and in your *left hand if you are right-handed*. Start in the upper corner.

Poke your needle through up from the back one hole in from your pencil marks in the top corner numbered 1 on the diagram (see Diagram 2). *Gently* pull the yarn through until one inch remains dangling on the reverse side. Hold this dangling end with your index finger against the back of the canvas. This loose end will be caught up and held down by your next stitches. Now, following the instructions, poke your needle down through the hole marked 2 on the diagram, and you have completed your first stitch. Think *diagonal*. Here are a couple of helpful hints: when going *up* on the diagonal, your *needle points directly right if you are left-handed* and *directly left if you are right-handed*; when coming down the row on the diagonal, your *needle points directly down*, whether left- or right-handed (see Diagram 3).

The most frustrating thing to learn is how to get around the corners to start a new row. Maybe this will help: when turning your top corner, you take the stitch that is *next to* the last stitch in your previous row. You always poke your needle up through the hole that is *one in* from your pencil line. When you stick your needle down through the pencil-lined hole, position your needle pointing *down*. When you turn your bottom corner, take the stitch directly *below* the last stitch in your previous row. Always poke your needle up through the hole that is *one in* from your pencil line. Then stick your

## BASKETWEAVE STITCH

### Diagram 2

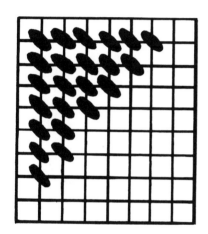

**Left-Handed**

| UP Through | DOWN Through |
|---|---|
| 1 | 2 |
| 3 | 4 |
| 5 | 6 |
| 7 | 8 |
| 9 | 1 |
| 10 | 11 |
| 12 | 13 |
| 14 | 3 |
| 15 | 5 |
| 16 | 17 |
| 18 | 19 |
| 20 | 7 |
| 21 | 9 |
| 22 | 10 |
| 23 | 24 |
| 25 | 26 |
| 27 | 12 |
| 28 | 14 |
| 29 | 15 |
| 30 | 16 |
| 31 | 32 |
| 33 | 34 |
| 35 | |

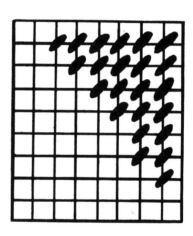

**Right-Handed**

## NEEDLE POSITIONS FOR
## BASKETWEAVE STITCH

### Diagram 3

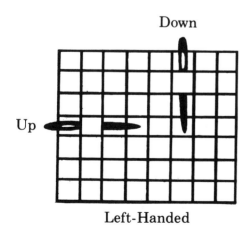

**Left-Handed**

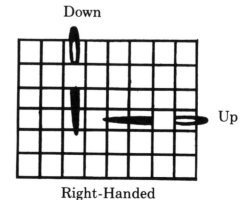

**Right-Handed**

needle down through the pencil-lined hole redirecting your needle to point directly *to the side*.

*Everyone makes mistakes,* not just beginners, and they can't be overlooked: they have to be taken out. Hopefully, they have not gotten out of hand. Minor surgery will be sufficient if there are only a couple of wrong stitches close together. Slip the needle off the sewing thread; working from the front, catch the needle under the stitch you last took, being careful not to hook the canvas, and pull up until the yarn slips through to the back and up through the front. Repeat this procedure until you have worked your way back to the point where your last correct stitch was taken. Re-thread your needle and you are ready to proceed. Now that was annoying, but relatively painless, and, best of all, no harm was done to the canvas.

Major surgery becomes necessary when there is no hope of working backward, undoing a stitch at a time. There is only one way to handle this situation—small sharp scissors, or better still, a seam ripper. Working from the front, *cautiously* slip the point of the open scissor *between* the canvas and the yarn. *Stop,* check to make absolutely sure that you are in the clear, and have not picked up one of the canvas threads. Cut through the wool. Continue along the row or rows, until you have snipped back to the correctly stitched area.

Turn the canvas over and catch your needle under the incorrect stitches previously snipped on the front side, and pull up. Lots of little yarn ends will pop out. Continue along until you have reached the correctly stitched area. Turn the canvas front side up, and pull out enough correct stitches to enable you to re-thread the needle and weave the end of the yarn into the back. This is without a doubt one of the most painful, aggravating, and frustrating procedures in needlepoint. What makes it doubly awful is that you are going backward. However, it is always worth it. Periodically look back over your work and check for mistakes, as it will save a lot of extra ripping if they are found early.

Following are thirty diagrams (numbered from 4-33 here and on corresponding charts) describing each stitch and showing its use in a stitchery patchwork pillow designed to incorporate all of these stitches, (see Plate 1).

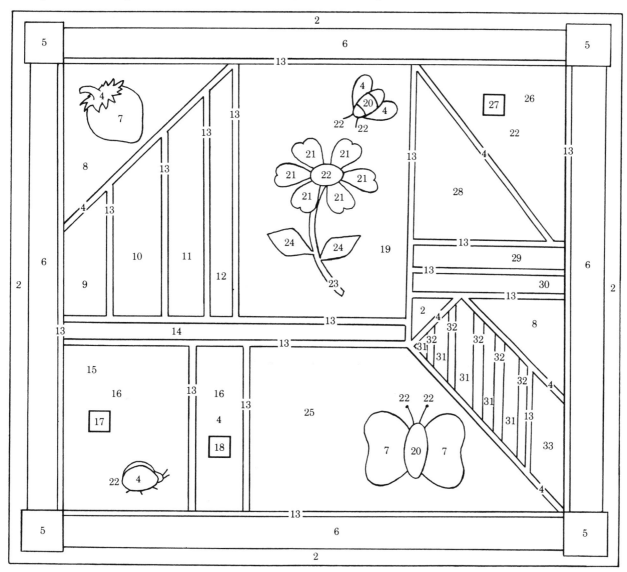

Diagram          Left-Handed (*See page 34 for Right-Handed Figure*).

4. Basketweave Stitch
5. Triangle Stitch
6. Pyramid Border Stitch
7. Strawberry Stitch
8. Gobelin Stitch
9. Parisian Stitch
10. Mosaic Stitch
11. Hungarian Stitch
12. Cashmere Stitch
13. Continental Stitch
14. Double Leviathan Stitch
15. Byzantine Stitch
16. Scotch Stitch
17. Byzantine and Scotch
18. Checkerboard of Basketweave and
    Counter Direction Scotch

19. Bargello
20. Surrey Stitch-Tufted
21. Interlocking Gobelin Stitch
22. French Knots
23. Satin Stitch
24. Leaf Stitch
25. Old Florentine Stitch
26. Slanting Gobelin Stitch
27. Slanting Horizontal Gobelin
    and French Knots
28. Diagonal Mosaic Stitch
29. Upright Knot Stitch
30. Smyrna Cross Stitch
31. Brick Stitch
32. Rice Stitch
33. Fern Stitch

Following are thirty diagrams (numbered from 4-33 here and on corresponding charts) describing each stitch and showing its use in a stitchery patchwork pillow designed to incorporate all of these stitches, (see Plate 1).

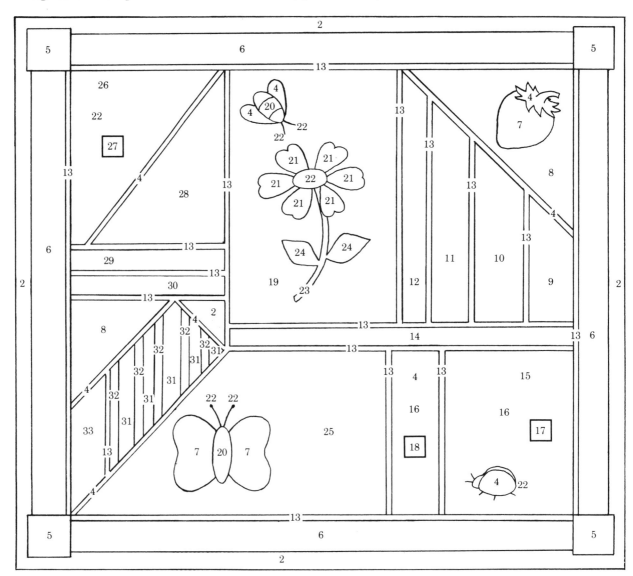

| Diagram | | Right-Handed | |
|---|---|---|---|
| 4. | Basketweave Stitch | 19. | Bargello |
| 5. | Triangle Stitch | 20. | Surrey Stitch-Tufted |
| 6. | Pyramid Border Stitch | 21. | Interlocking Gobelin Stitch |
| 7. | Strawberry Stitch | 22. | French Knots |
| 8. | Gobelin Stitch | 23. | Satin Stitch |
| 9. | Parisian Stitch | 24. | Leaf Stitch |
| 10. | Mosaic Stitch | 25. | Old Florentine Stitch |
| 11. | Hungarian Stitch | 26. | Slanting Gobelin Stitch |
| 12. | Cashmere Stitch | 27. | Slanting Horizontal Gobelin |
| 13. | Continental Stitch | | and French Knots |
| 14. | Double Leviathan Stitch | 28. | Diagonal Mosaic Stitch |
| 15. | Byzantine Stitch | 29. | Upright Knot Stitch |
| 16. | Scotch Stitch | 30. | Smyrna Cross Stitch |
| 17. | Byzantine and Scotch | 31. | Brick Stitch |
| 18. | Checkerboard of Basketweave and | 32. | Rice Stitch |
| | Counter Direction Scotch | 33. | Fern Stitch |

***Basketweave Stitch.*** Single diagonal rows worked with 2 threads. Use 2 threads 4 rows wide to surround Pyramid Border Stitch and 3 rows wide to surround Triangle Stitch corners (this is added after the rest of the pillow has been stitched, see Diagram 2).

Diagram 4

| UP Through | DOWN Through |
|:---:|:---:|
| 1 ———————— | 2 |
| 3 ———————— | 4 |
| 5 ———————— | 6 |
| 7 ———————— | 8 |
| 9 ———————— | 10 |
| 11 ———————— | 12 |
| 13 ———————— | 14 |
| 15 ———————— | 13 |
| 16 ———————— | 15 |
| 17 ———————— | 16 |
| 18 ———————— | 17 |
| 19 ———————— | 18 |
| 20 ———————— | 19 |

Left-Handed

*(see page 36 for Right-Handed Diagram)*

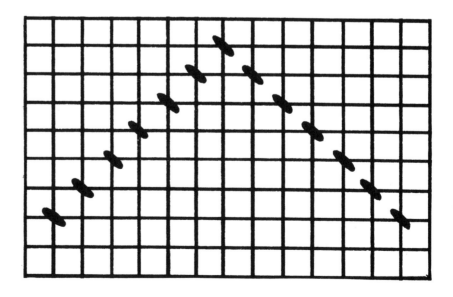

***Basketweave Stitch.*** Single diagonal rows worked with 2 threads. Use 2 threads 4 rows wide to surround Pyramid Border Stitch and 3 rows wide to surround Triangle Stitch corners (this is added after the rest of the pillow has been stitched, see Diagram 2).

Diagram 4

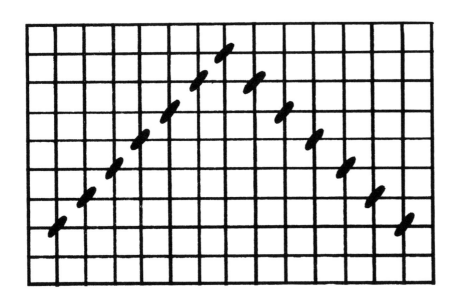

Right-Handed

| UP Through | DOWN Through |
|---|---|
| 1 ———————— | 2 |
| 3 ———————— | 4 |
| 5 ———————— | 6 |
| 7 ———————— | 8 |
| 9 ———————— | 10 |
| 11 ———————— | 12 |
| 13 ———————— | 14 |
| 15 ———————— | 13 |
| 16 ———————— | 15 |
| 17 ———————— | 16 |
| 18 ———————— | 17 |
| 19 ———————— | 18 |
| 20 ———————— | 19 |

***Triangle Stitch.*** Worked with as whole strand. This can be the icing on the cake. Placed at the corners of a design with a pattern border, it gives the piece a finished look.

Diagram 5

| 2 | 4 | 45 | 44 | 43 | 42 | 41 | 40 | 37 |
|---|---|---|---|---|---|---|---|---|
| 3 | 1 |   |   |   |   |   | 38 | 39 |
| 6 |   | 5 |   |   |   | 36 |   | 35 |
| 8 |   |   | 7 |   | 34 |   |   | 33 |
| 10 |   |   |   | 9 |   |   |   | 32 |
| 12 |   |   | 11 |   | 23 |   |   | 31 |
| 14 |   | 13 |   |   |   | 25 |   | 30 |
| 16 | 18 |   |   |   |   |   | 29 | 27 |
| 17 | 15 | 19 | 20 | 21 | 22 | 24 | 26 | 28 |

This stitch is used mostly for corners. However, if used as a border pattern, the left-hander counts 5 stitches to the right and 5 stitches down to start the next triangle. The right-hander counts 5 stitches to the left and 5 stitches down to start the next triangle.

| UP Through | DOWN Through |
|---|---|
| 1 | 2 |
| 3 | 4 |
| 5 | 6 |
| 7 | 8 |
| 9 | 10 |
| 11 | 12 |
| 13 | 14 |
| 15 | 16 |
| 17 | 18 |
| 19 | 13 |
| 20 | 11 |
| 21 | 9 |
| 22 | 23 |
| 24 | 25 |
| 26 | 27 |
| 28 | 29 |
| 30 | 25 |
| 31 | 23 |
| 32 | 9 |
| 33 | 34 |
| 35 | 36 |
| 37 | 38 |
| 39 | 40 |
| 36 | 41 |
| 34 | 42 |
| 9 | 43 |
| 7 | 44 |
| 5 | 45 |

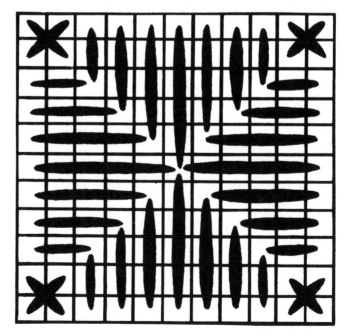

Left-Handed

*(see page 38 for Right-Handed Diagram)*

***Triangle Stitch.*** Worked with as whole strand. This can be the icing on the cake. Placed at the corners of a design with a pattern border, it gives the piece a finished look.

Diagram 5

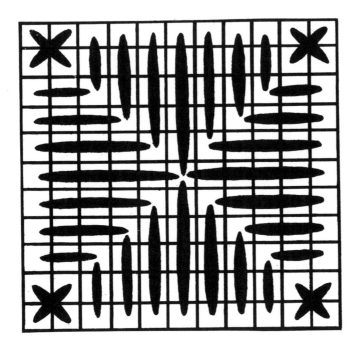

| 37 | 40 | 41 | 42 | 43 | 44 | 45 | 4  | 2  |
|----|----|----|----|----|----|----|----|----|
| 39 | 38 |    |    |    |    |    | 1  | 3  |
| 35 |    | 36 |    |    |    | 5  |    | 6  |
| 33 |    |    | 34 |    | 7  |    |    | 8  |
| 32 |    |    |    | 9  |    |    |    | 10 |
| 31 |    |    | 23 |    | 11 |    |    | 12 |
| 30 |    | 25 |    |    |    | 13 |    | 14 |
| 27 | 29 |    |    |    |    |    | 18 | 16 |
| 28 | 26 | 24 | 22 | 21 | 20 | 19 | 15 | 17 |

Right-Handed

This stitch is used mostly for corners. However, if used as a border pattern, the left-hander counts 5 stitches to the right and 5 stitches down to start the next triangle. The right-hander counts 5 stitches to the left and 5 stitches down to start the next triangle.

| UP Through | | DOWN Through |
|---|---|---|
| 1 | ——————— | 2 |
| 3 | ——————— | 4 |
| 5 | ——————— | 6 |
| 7 | ——————— | 8 |
| 9 | ——————— | 10 |
| 11 | ——————— | 12 |
| 13 | ——————— | 14 |
| 15 | ——————— | 16 |
| 17 | ——————— | 18 |
| 19 | ——————— | 13 |
| 20 | ——————— | 11 |
| 21 | ——————— | 9 |
| 22 | ——————— | 23 |
| 24 | ——————— | 25 |
| 26 | ——————— | 27 |
| 28 | ——————— | 29 |
| 30 | ——————— | 25 |
| 31 | ——————— | 23 |
| 32 | ——————— | 9 |
| 33 | ——————— | 34 |
| 35 | ——————— | 36 |
| 37 | ——————— | 38 |
| 39 | ——————— | 40 |
| 36 | ——————— | 41 |
| 34 | ——————— | 42 |
| 9 | ——————— | 43 |
| 7 | ——————— | 44 |
| 5 | ——————— | 45 |

**Pyramid Border Stitch.** Worked with 2 threads. 18 units* across and 16 units down. This is an elegant border. It is essential to count this out before filling in the background or Stitchery center.

Diagram 6

**Left-Handed**

| 46 | 2 | 4 | 6 | 8 | 10 | 12 | 14 | 38 | 16 | 18 | 20 | 22 | 24 | 26 | 28 | 30 |
|----|---|---|---|---|----|----|----|----|----|----|----|----|----|----|----|----|
|  | 1 |  |  |  |  |  | 13 |  | 15 |  |  |  |  |  | 27 |  |
|  |  | 3 |  |  |  | 11 |  |  |  | 17 |  |  |  | 25 |  |  |
|  |  |  | 5 |  | 9 |  |  |  |  |  | 19 |  | 23 |  |  |  |
| 45 | 44 | 43 | 42 | 7 | 41 | 40 | 39 | 37 | 36 | 35 | 34 | 21 | 33 | 32 | 31 | 29 |
|  | 47 |  |  |  |  |  |  | 53 |  | 54 |  |  |  |  | 60 |  |
|  |  | 48 |  |  |  | 52 |  |  |  | 55 |  |  |  | 59 |  |  |
|  |  |  | 49 |  | 51 |  |  |  |  |  | 56 |  | 58 |  |  |  |
|  |  |  |  | 50 |  |  |  |  |  |  |  | 57 |  |  |  | 61 |

**Right-Handed**

| 30 | 28 | 26 | 24 | 22 | 20 | 18 | 16 | 38 | 14 | 12 | 10 | 8 | 6 | 4 | 2 | 46 |
|----|----|----|----|----|----|----|----|----|----|----|----|---|---|---|---|----|
|  | 27 |  |  |  |  | 15 |  |  | 13 |  |  |  |  |  | 1 |  |
|  |  | 25 |  |  |  | 17 |  |  |  | 11 |  |  |  | 3 |  |  |
|  |  |  | 23 |  | 19 |  |  |  |  |  | 9 |  | 5 |  |  |  |
| 29 | 31 | 32 | 33 | 21 | 34 | 35 | 36 | 37 | 39 | 40 | 41 | 7 | 42 | 43 | 44 | 45 |
|  | 60 |  |  |  |  |  |  | 54 |  | 53 |  |  |  |  | 47 |  |
|  |  | 59 |  |  |  | 55 |  |  |  | 52 |  |  |  | 48 |  |  |
|  |  |  | 58 |  | 56 |  |  |  |  |  | 51 |  | 49 |  |  |  |
| 61 |  |  |  | 57 |  |  |  |  |  |  |  | 50 |  |  |  |  |

**Right- and Left-Handed**

| UP Through | DOWN Through |
|------------|--------------|
| 1 | 2 |
| 3 | 4 |
| 5 | 6 |
| 7 | 8 |
| 9 | 10 |
| 11 | 12 |
| 13 | 14 |
| 15 | 16 |
| 17 | 18 |
| 19 | 20 |
| 21 | 22 |
| 23 | 24 |
| 25 | 26 |
| 27 | 28 |
| 29 | 30 |
| 31 | 27 |
| 32 | 25 |
| 33 | 23 |
| 34 | 19 |
| 35 | 17 |
| 36 | 15 |
| 37 | 38 |
| 39 | 13 |
| 40 | 11 |
| 41 | 9 |
| 42 | 5 |
| 43 | 3 |
| 44 | 1 |
| 45 | 46 |
| 47 | 44 |
| 48 | 43 |
| 49 | 42 |
| 50 | 7 |
| 51 | 41 |
| 52 | 40 |
| 53 | 39 |
| 54 | 36 |
| 55 | 35 |
| 56 | 34 |
| 57 | 21 |
| 58 | 33 |
| 59 | 32 |
| 60 | 31 |
| 61 |  |

* The term "unit" means a completed group of stitches that comprise a pattern, i.e., the short-long-short combination in the Hungarian Stitch.

***Strawberry Stitch.*** Worked with 2 threads. Top of strawberry in Basketweave. This stitch resembles the texture of a strawberry, which is how it came by its name. It is a handsome, speedy stitch (see Figure 4).

Diagram 7

| UP Through | DOWN Through |
|---|---|
| 1 ——————— 2 |  |
| 3 ——————— 4 |  |
| 5 ——————— 6 |  |
| 7 ——————— 8 |  |
| 9 ——————— 10 |  |
| 11 ——————— 12 |  |
| 13 ——————— 1 |  |
| 14 ——————— 15 |  |
| 16 ——————— 17 |  |
| 18 ——————— 19 |  |
| 20 ——————— 21 |  |
| 22 ——————— 16 |  |
| 23 ——————— 3 |  |
| 24 ——————— 5 |  |
| 25 ——————— 7 |  |
| 26 ——————— 27 |  |
| 28 ——————— 29 |  |
| 30 ——————— 19 |  |
| 31 ——————— 11 |  |
| 32 ——————— 13 |  |
| 33 ——————— 14 |  |
| 34 ——————— 18 |  |
| 35 ——————— 36 |  |
| 37 ——————— 38 |  |
| 39 ——————— 40 |  |
| 41 ——————— 42 |  |
| 43 ——————— 37 |  |
| 44 |  |

| 2 | 4 | 15 | 17 | 19 | 21 | 36 | 38 | 40 | 42 |  |  |
|---|---|---|---|---|---|---|---|---|---|---|---|
| 6 | 1 |  |  | 16 | 18 |  |  | 37 | 39 |  |  |
| 12 |  |  | 3 | 14 |  |  | 20 | 35 |  |  | 41 |
| 8 |  | 5 | 13 |  |  | 22 | 34 |  |  | 43 |  |
| 10 | 7 | 11 |  |  | 23 | 33 |  |  | 44 |  |  |
| 27 | 9 |  |  | 24 | 32 |  |  |  |  |  |  |
| 29 |  |  | 25 | 31 |  |  |  |  |  |  |  |
|  |  | 26 | 30 |  |  |  |  |  |  |  |  |
|  |  | 28 |  |  |  |  |  |  |  |  |  |

Left-Handed

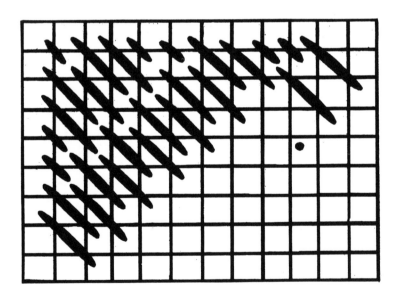

Figure 4

Left-Handed

***Strawberry Stitch.*** Worked with 2 threads. Top of strawberry in Basketweave. This stitch resembles the texture of a strawberry, which is how it came by its name. It is a handsome, speedy stitch (see Figure 4).

Diagram 7

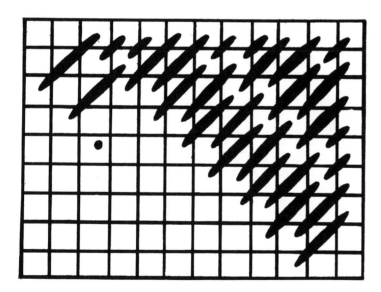

| | | | | | | | | | | | |
|---|---|---|---|---|---|---|---|---|---|---|---|
| | | 42 | 40 | 38 | 36 | 21 | 19 | 17 | 15 | 4 | 2 |
| | | 39 | 37 | | | 18 | 16 | | | 1 | 6 |
| 41 | | | 35 | 20 | | | 14 | 3 | | | 12 |
| | 43 | | | 34 | 22 | | | 13 | 5 | | 8 |
| | | 44 | | | 33 | 23 | | | 11 | 7 | 10 |
| | | | | | | 32 | 24 | | | 9 | 27 |
| | | | | | | | 31 | 25 | | | 29 |
| | | | | | | | | 30 | 26 | | |
| | | | | | | | | | 28 | | |
| | | | | | | | | | | | |

Right-Handed

| UP Through | DOWN Through |
|---|---|
| 1 ——————— | 2 |
| 3 ——————— | 4 |
| 5 ——————— | 6 |
| 7 ——————— | 8 |
| 9 ——————— | 10 |
| 11 ——————— | 12 |
| 13 ——————— | 1 |
| 14 ——————— | 15 |
| 16 ——————— | 17 |
| 18 ——————— | 19 |
| 20 ——————— | 21 |
| 22 ——————— | 16 |
| 23 ——————— | 3 |
| 24 ——————— | 5 |
| 25 ——————— | 7 |
| 26 ——————— | 27 |
| 28 ——————— | 29 |
| 30 ——————— | 19 |
| 31 ——————— | 11 |
| 32 ——————— | 13 |
| 33 ——————— | 14 |
| 34 ——————— | 18 |
| 35 ——————— | 36 |
| 37 ——————— | 38 |
| 39 ——————— | 40 |
| 41 ——————— | 42 |
| 43 ——————— | 37 |
| 44 | |

Figure 4

Right-Handed

***Gobelin Stitch.*** Worked over 4 rows of canvas using 1 strand. 48 rows across and 48 rows down (or 12 units). Behind the strawberry.

Worked over 2 canvas rows with 2 threads. 33 rows across and 32 rows down (or 16 units). Section under Smyrna Cross Stitch.

For the first time, you will be working your stitches straight up and down to form this neat pattern.

## Diagram 8

| | UP Through | DOWN Through |
|---|---|---|
| 1 | ——————— | 2 |
| 3 | ——————— | 4 |
| 5 | ——————— | 6 |
| 7 | ——————— | 8 |
| 9 | ——————— | 10 |
| 11 | ——————— | 12 |
| 13 | ——————— | 14 |
| 15 | ——————— | 16 |
| 17 | ——————— | 18 |
| 19 | ——————— | 17 |
| 20 | ——————— | 15 |
| 21 | ——————— | 13 |
| 22 | ——————— | 11 |
| 23 | ——————— | 9 |
| 24 | ——————— | 7 |
| 25 | ——————— | 5 |
| 26 | ——————— | 3 |
| 27 | ——————— | 1 |
| 28 | | |

**Left-Handed grid:**

| 2 | 4 | 6 | 8 | 10 | 12 | 14 | 16 | 18 |
|---|---|---|---|---|---|---|---|---|
| | | | | | | | | |
| 1 | 3 | 5 | 7 | 9 | 11 | 13 | 15 | 17 |
| | | | | | | | | |
| 27 | 26 | 25 | 24 | 23 | 22 | 21 | 20 | 19 |
| | | | | | | | | |
| 28 | | | | | | | | |

Left-Handed

**Right-Handed grid:**

| 18 | 16 | 14 | 12 | 10 | 8 | 6 | 4 | 2 |
|---|---|---|---|---|---|---|---|---|
| | | | | | | | | |
| 17 | 15 | 13 | 11 | 9 | 7 | 5 | 3 | |
| | | | | | | | | |
| 19 | 20 | 21 | 22 | 23 | 24 | 25 | 26 | |
| | | | | | | | | |
| | | | | | | | | 28 |

Right-Handed

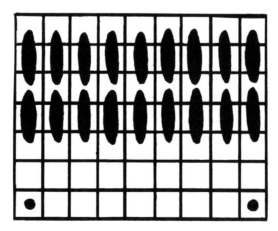

Right- and Left-Handed

***Parisian Stitch.*** Worked with 2 threads. 23 rows down and 6 units across. The 23rd row down is a fill-in row of single stitches and 6½ units across or 13 stitches. This is a very tidy, easy-flowing background stitch.

Diagram 9

| UP Through | DOWN Through |
|:---:|:---:|
| 1 —————— | 2 |
| 3 —————— | 4 |
| 5 —————— | 6 |
| 7 —————— | 8 |
| 9 —————— | 10 |
| 11 —————— | 12 |
| 13 —————— | 14 |
| 15 —————— | 16 |
| 17 —————— | 15 |
| 18 —————— | 13 |
| 19 —————— | 11 |
| 20 —————— | 9 |
| 21 —————— | 7 |
| 22 —————— | 5 |
| 23 —————— | 3 |
| 24 —————— | 1 |
| 25 | |

Left-Handed

*(see page 44 for Right-Handed Diagram)*

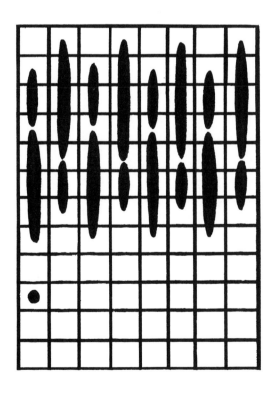

***Parisian Stitch.*** Worked with 2 threads. 23 rows down and 6 units across. The 23rd row down is a fill-in row of single stitches and 6½ units across or 13 stitches. This is a very tidy, easy-flowing background stitch.

Diagram 9

| | 14 | | 10 | | 6 | | 2 |
|---|---|---|---|---|---|---|---|
| 16 | | 12 | | 8 | | 4 | |
| | | | | | | | |
| 15 | | 11 | | 7 | | 3 | |
| | 13 | | 9 | | 5 | | 1 |
| | | | | | | | |
| | 18 | | 20 | | 22 | | 24 |
| 17 | | 19 | | 21 | | 23 | |
| | | | | | | | |
| | | | | | | | |
| | | | | | | | 25 |
| | | | | | | | |

Right-Handed

| UP Through | | DOWN Through |
|---|---|---|
| 1 | ——————— | 2 |
| 3 | ——————— | 4 |
| 5 | ——————— | 6 |
| 7 | ——————— | 8 |
| 9 | ——————— | 10 |
| 11 | ——————— | 12 |
| 13 | ——————— | 14 |
| 15 | ——————— | 16 |
| 17 | ——————— | 15 |
| 18 | ——————— | 13 |
| 19 | ——————— | 11 |
| 20 | ——————— | 9 |
| 21 | ——————— | 7 |
| 22 | ——————— | 5 |
| 23 | ——————— | 3 |
| 24 | ——————— | 1 |
| 25 | | |

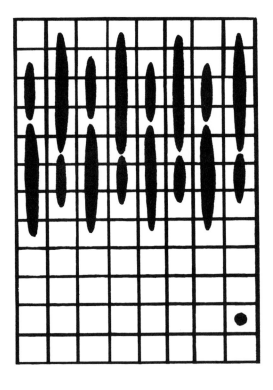

**Mosaic Stitch.** Worked with 2 threads. 18 units down (short side), 8 units across. Though at first glance it looks like a Cross Stitch, it is not. It is tight, and is one of the few stitches that can be used on a rug and withstand the wear. This stitch can be done as shown here in two different colors, forming a pattern-within-a-pattern.

Diagram 10

| UP Through | | DOWN Through |
|---|---|---|
| 1 | ———— | 2 |
| 3 | ———— | 4 |
| 5 | ———— | 6 |
| 7 | ———— | 8 |
| 9 | ———— | 10 |
| 11 | ———— | 5 |
| 12 | ———— | 1 |
| 13 | ———— | 14 |
| 15 | ———— | 16 |
| 17 | ———— | 18 |
| 19 | ———— | 20 |
| 21 | ———— | 15 |
| 22 | ———— | 12 |
| 23 | ———— | 3 |
| 24 | ———— | 11 |
| 25 | ———— | 7 |
| 26 | ———— | 27 |
| 28 | ———— | 29 |
| 30 | ———— | 31 |
| 32 | ———— | 33 |
| 34 | ———— | 28 |
| 35 | ———— | 25 |
| 36 | ———— | 9 |
| 37 | ———— | 24 |
| 38 | ———— | 22 |
| 39 | ———— | 13 |
| 40 | ———— | 21 |
| 41 | ———— | 17 |
| 42 | ———— | 43 |
| 44 | ———— | 45 |
| 46 | ———— | 47 |

| 4 | 6 | 10 | 8 | 27 | 29 | 33 | 31 | |
|---|---|---|---|---|---|---|---|---|
| 2 | | 5 | | 7 | | 28 | | 30 |
| 14 | 1 | 3 | 11 | 9 | 25 | 26 | 34 | 32 |
| 16 | | 12 | | 24 | | 35 | | |
| 20 | 15 | 13 | 22 | 23 | 37 | 36 | | |
| 18 | | 21 | | 38 | | | | |
| 43 | 17 | 19 | 40 | 39 | | | | |
| 45 | | 41 | | | | | | |
| | 44 | 42 | | | | | | |
| 47 | | | | | | | | |
| | 46 | | | | | | | |

Left-Handed

*(see page 46 for Right-Handed Diagram)*

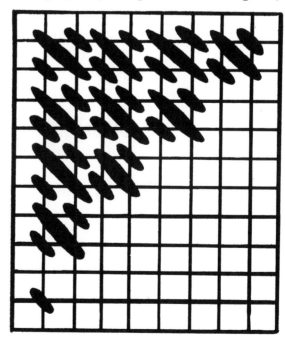

**Mosaic Stitch.** Worked with 2 threads. 18 units down (short side), 8 units across. Though at first glance it looks like a Cross Stitch, it is not. It is tight, and is one of the few stitches that can be used on a rug and withstand the wear. This stitch can be done as shown here in two different colors, forming a pattern-within-a-pattern.

Diagram 10

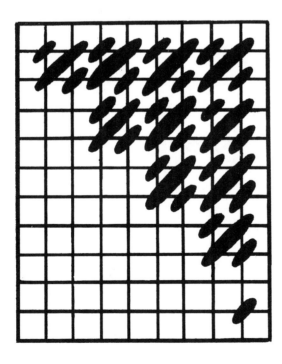

Right-Handed

| UP Through | | DOWN Through |
|---|---|---|
| 1 | ——————— | 2 |
| 3 | ——————— | 4 |
| 5 | ——————— | 6 |
| 7 | ——————— | 8 |
| 9 | ——————— | 10 |
| 11 | ——————— | 5 |
| 12 | ——————— | 1 |
| 13 | ——————— | 14 |
| 15 | ——————— | 16 |
| 17 | ——————— | 18 |
| 19 | ——————— | 20 |
| 21 | ——————— | 15 |
| 22 | ——————— | 12 |
| 23 | ——————— | 3 |
| 24 | ——————— | 11 |
| 25 | ——————— | 7 |
| 26 | ——————— | 27 |
| 28 | ——————— | 29 |
| 30 | ——————— | 31 |
| 32 | ——————— | 33 |
| 34 | ——————— | 28 |
| 35 | ——————— | 25 |
| 36 | ——————— | 9 |
| 37 | ——————— | 24 |
| 38 | ——————— | 22 |
| 39 | ——————— | 13 |
| 40 | ——————— | 21 |
| 41 | ——————— | 17 |
| 42 | ——————— | 43 |
| 44 | ——————— | 45 |
| 46 | ——————— | 47 |

**Hungarian Stitch.** Worked with 2 threads. 26 units plus 1 row or 53 rows down (short side). 4 units across. Very similar to the Parisian in that it is made up of a short-long-short combination of stitches. The difference is in the formation of short-long-short units that are separated in the Hungarian, unlike those in the Parisian.

Diagram 11

UP Through     DOWN Through

| UP Through | | DOWN Through |
|---|---|---|
| 1 | ————————— | 2 |
| 3 | ————————— | 4 |
| 5 | ————————— | 6 |
| 7 | ————————— | 8 |
| 9 | ————————— | 10 |
| 11 | ————————— | 12 |
| 13 | ————————— | 14 |
| 15 | ————————— | 16 |
| 17 | ————————— | 18 |
| 19 | ————————— | 17 |
| 20 | ————————— | 13 |
| 21 | ————————— | 22 |
| 23 | ————————— | 11 |
| 24 | ————————— | 7 |
| 25 | ————————— | 26 |
| 27 | ————————— | 5 |
| 28 | ————————— | 1 |
| 29 | ————————— | 28 |
| 30 | ————————— | 3 |
| 31 | ————————— | 27 |
| 32 | ————————— | 24 |
| 33 | ————————— | 9 |
| 34 | ————————— | 23 |
| 35 | ————————— | 20 |
| 36 | ————————— | 15 |
| 37 | ————————— | 19 |
| 38 | | |

Left-Handed

Right-Handed

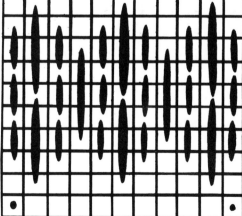

Right- and Left-Handed

***Cashmere Stitch.*** Worked with 2 threads. 22 units down, the 23rd unit down is a Mosaic (short side). 3 units across. This is an elongated version of the Mosaic and the Scotch. It can be done in one solid color, or two different colors can be used on alternate boxes, forming a pattern-within-a-pattern.

Diagram 12

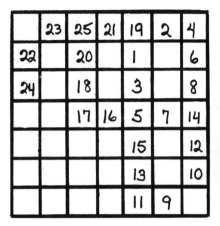

| UP Through | | DOWN Through |
|---|---|---|
| 1 | —————— | 2 |
| 3 | —————— | 4 |
| 5 | —————— | 6 |
| 7 | —————— | 8 |
| 9 | —————— | 10 |
| 11 | —————— | 12 |
| 13 | —————— | 14 |
| 15 | —————— | 7 |
| 16 | —————— | 3 |
| 17 | —————— | 1 |
| 18 | —————— | 19 |
| 20 | —————— | 21 |
| 22 | —————— | 23 |
| 24 | —————— | 25 |

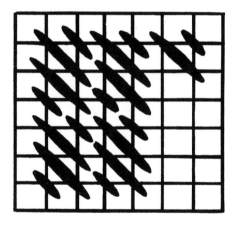

Left-Handed

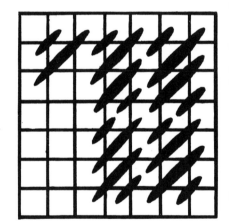

Right-Handed

***Continental Stitch.*** Worked with 2 threads. Single rows separating pattern stitches. Single line shown here is the Continental going down a row, and across.

Diagram 13

| UP Through | DOWN Through |
|---|---|
| 1 ———————— | 2 |
| 3 ———————— | 4 |
| 5 ———————— | 6 |
| 7 ———————— | 8 |
| 9 ———————— | 10 |
| 11 ———————— | 12 |
| 13 ———————— | 14 |
| 15 ———————— | 11 |
| 16 ———————— | 17 |
| 18 ———————— | 19 |
| 20 ———————— | 21 |

Left-Handed

Right-Handed

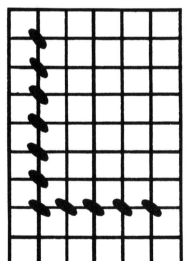

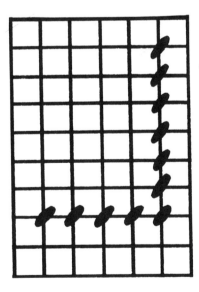

***Double Leviathan Stitch.*** Worked with 2 threads. 23 units across. A compact, bumpy stitch that can easily be incorporated into a border. As shown here, it can be done in alternating colors.

Diagram 14

| | | | | | | | | | | | | |
|---|---|---|---|---|---|---|---|---|---|---|---|---|
| 2 | 8 | 14 | 6 | 4 | 33 | 37 | 31 | 29 | | | | |
| 12 | | | | 9 | | | | 34 | | | | |
| 16 | | | | 15 | | | | 38 | | | | |
| 10 | | | | 11 | | | | 35 | | | | |
| 3 | 5 | 13 | 7 | 1 | 30 | 36 | 32 | 28 | | | | 39 |
| 24 | | | | 21 | | | | | | | | |
| 27 | | | | 26 | | | | | | | | |
| 22 | | | | 23 | | | | | | | | |
| 18 | 19 | 25 | 20 | 17 | | | | | | | | |

| UP Through | DOWN Through |
|---|---|
| 1 | 2 |
| 3 | 4 |
| 5 | 6 |
| 7 | 8 |
| 9 | 10 |
| 11 | 12 |
| 13 | 14 |
| 15 | 16 |

This completes unit one.

| | |
|---|---|
| 17 | 3 |
| 18 | 1 |
| 19 | 7 |
| 20 | 5 |
| 21 | 22 |
| 23 | 24 |
| 25 | 13 |
| 26 | 27 |

This completes unit two.

| | |
|---|---|
| 28 | 4 |
| 1 | 29 |
| 30 | 31 |
| 32 | 33 |
| 34 | 11 |
| 35 | 9 |
| 36 | 37 |
| 38 | 15 |

This completes unit three.

39

Left-Handed

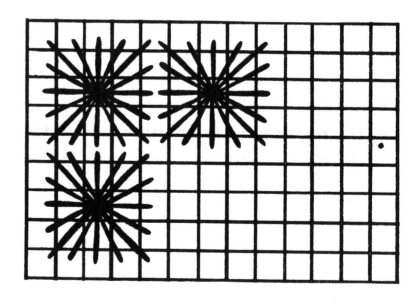

***Double Leviathan Stitch.*** Worked with 2 threads. 23 units across. A compact, bumpy stitch that can easily be incorporated into a border. As shown here, it can be done in alternating colors.

Diagram 14

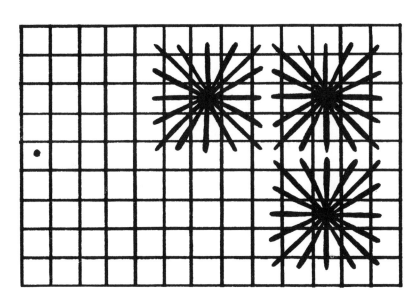

Right-Handed

| UP Through | DOWN Through |
|---|---|
| 1 ——————— | 2 |
| 3 ——————— | 4 |
| 5 ——————— | 6 |
| 7 ——————— | 8 |
| 9 ——————— | 10 |
| 11 ——————— | 12 |
| 13 ——————— | 14 |
| 15 ——————— | 16 |

This completes unit one.

| UP Through | DOWN Through |
|---|---|
| 17 ——————— | 3 |
| 18 ——————— | 1 |
| 19 ——————— | 7 |
| 20 ——————— | 5 |
| 21 ——————— | 22 |
| 23 ——————— | 24 |
| 25 ——————— | 13 |
| 26 ——————— | 27 |

This completes unit two.

| UP Through | DOWN Through |
|---|---|
| 28 ——————— | 4 |
| 1 ——————— | 29 |
| 30 ——————— | 31 |
| 32 ——————— | 33 |
| 34 ——————— | 11 |
| 35 ——————— | 9 |
| 36 ——————— | 37 |
| 38 ——————— | 15 |

This completes unit three.

39

***Byzantine Stitch.*** Worked with 2 threads. This is one of the most dramatic and stylish stitches. It has to be worked in large areas to be effective.

Diagram 15

| UP Through | DOWN Through |
|---|---|
| 1 ———————— 2 |
| 3 ———————— 4 |
| 5 ———————— 6 |
| 7 ———————— 8 |
| 9 ———————— 10 |
| 11 ———————— 12 |
| 13 ———————— 14 |
| 15 ———————— 16 |
| 17 ———————— 18 |
| 19 ———————— 20 |
| 21 ———————— 22 |
| 23 ———————— 24 |
| 25 ———————— 26 |
| 27 ———————— 28 |
| 29 ———————— 30 |
| 31 ———————— 32 |
| 33 ———————— 25 |
| 34 ———————— 23 |
| 35 ———————— 21 |
| 36 ———————— 19 |
| 37 ———————— 17 |
| 38 ———————— 15 |
| 39 ———————— 13 |
| 40 ———————— 11 |
| 41 ———————— 9 |
| 42 ———————— 7 |
| 43 ———————— 5 |
| 44 ———————— 3 |
| 45 ———————— 1 |
| 46 ———————— 47 |
| 48 ———————— 49 |
| 50 ———————— 51 |
| 52 ———————— 53 |
| 54 ———————— 55 |
| 56 ———————— 57 |
| 58 |

Left-Handed

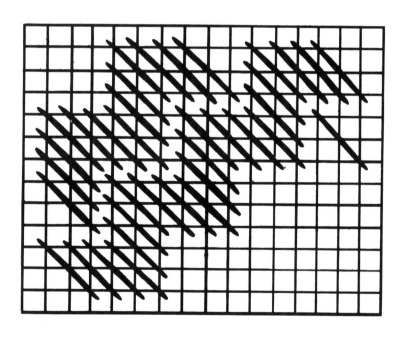

**Byzantine Stitch.** Worked with 2 threads. This is one of the most dramatic and stylish stitches. It has to be worked in large areas to be effective.

Diagram 15

|  |  |  |  |  |  |  |  |  |  |  |  |  |  |
|---|---|---|---|---|---|---|---|---|---|---|---|---|---|
|  |  | 57 | 55 | 53 | 51 |  |  | 2 | 4 | 6 | 8 |  |  |
|  |  |  |  |  | 49 |  |  |  |  |  | 10 |  |  |
|  |  |  |  |  | 47 |  |  |  |  |  | 12 |  |  |
| 56 | 54 | 52 | 50 |  | 1 | 3 | 5 | 7 |  | 14 | 16 | 18 | 20 |
|  |  |  | 48 |  |  |  |  | 9 |  |  |  |  | 22 |
|  |  |  | 46 |  |  |  |  | 11 |  |  |  |  | 24 |
| 58 |  |  | 45 | 44 | 43 | 42 |  | 13 | 15 | 17 | 19 |  | 26 |
|  |  |  |  |  |  | 41 |  |  |  |  | 21 |  |  |
|  |  |  |  |  |  | 40 |  |  |  |  | 23 |  |  |
|  |  |  |  |  |  | 39 | 38 | 37 | 36 | 25 | 32 | 30 | 28 |
|  |  |  |  |  |  |  |  |  | 35 |  |  |  |  |
|  |  |  |  |  |  |  |  |  | 34 |  |  |  |  |
|  |  |  |  |  |  |  |  |  | 33 | 31 | 29 | 27 |  |

Right-Handed

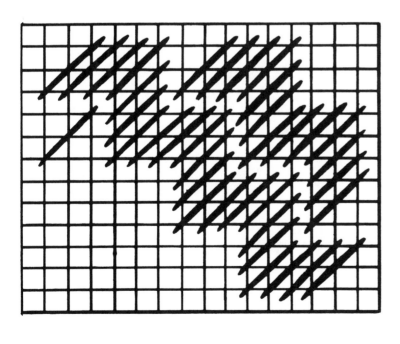

| UP Through | DOWN Through |
|---|---|
| 1 | 2 |
| 3 | 4 |
| 5 | 6 |
| 7 | 8 |
| 9 | 10 |
| 11 | 12 |
| 13 | 14 |
| 15 | 16 |
| 17 | 18 |
| 19 | 20 |
| 21 | 22 |
| 23 | 24 |
| 25 | 26 |
| 27 | 28 |
| 29 | 30 |
| 31 | 32 |
| 33 | 25 |
| 34 | 23 |
| 35 | 21 |
| 36 | 19 |
| 37 | 17 |
| 38 | 15 |
| 39 | 13 |
| 40 | 11 |
| 41 | 9 |
| 42 | 7 |
| 43 | 5 |
| 44 | 3 |
| 45 | 1 |
| 46 | 47 |
| 48 | 49 |
| 50 | 51 |
| 52 | 53 |
| 54 | 55 |
| 56 | 57 |
| 58 |  |

**Scotch Stitch.** Worked with 2 threads. A delightfully adaptable stitch. It can be done in one solid color, or two different ones. It can also be done in units, facing each other, i.e., one box of stitches slanting to the right, and the next slanting to the left.

Diagram 16

| 8 | 10 | 12 | 14 | 22 | 20 | 18 | 16 | |
|---|---|---|---|---|---|---|---|---|
| 6 | | | | 13 | | | | 15 |
| 4 | | | | 11 | | | | 17 |
| 2 | | | | 9 | | | | 19 |
| 30 | 1 | 3 | 5 | 7 | 25 | 24 | 23 | 21 |
| 32 | | | | 26 | | | | |
| 34 | | | | 27 | | | | |
| 36 | | | | 28 | | | | |
| | 35 | 33 | 31 | 29 | | | | |
| | | | | | | | | |
| | | | | | | | | |
| 38 | | | | | | | | |
| | 37 | | | | | | | |

Left-Handed

| UP Through | DOWN Through |
|---|---|
| 1 ——————— | 2 |
| 3 ——————— | 4 |
| 5 ——————— | 6 |
| 7 ——————— | 8 |
| 9 ——————— | 10 |
| 11 ——————— | 12 |
| 13 ——————— | 14 |
| 15 ——————— | 16 |
| 17 ——————— | 18 |
| 19 ——————— | 20 |
| 21 ——————— | 22 |
| 23 ——————— | 13 |
| 24 ——————— | 11 |
| 25 ——————— | 9 |
| 26 ——————— | 5 |
| 27 ——————— | 3 |
| 28 ——————— | 1 |
| 29 ——————— | 30 |
| 31 ——————— | 32 |
| 33 ——————— | 34 |
| 35 ——————— | 36 |
| 37 ——————— | 38 |

**_Scotch Stitch._** Worked with 2 threads. A delightfully adaptable stitch. It can be done in one solid color, or two different ones. It can also be done in units, facing each other, i.e., one box of stitches slanting to the right, and the next slanting to the left.

Diagram 16

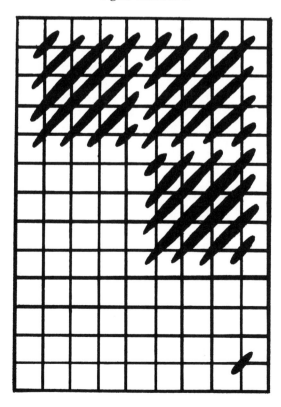

| | 16 | 18 | 20 | 22 | 14 | 12 | 10 | 8 |
|---|---|---|---|---|---|---|---|---|
| 15 | | | | 13 | | | | 6 |
| 17 | | | | 11 | | | | 4 |
| 19 | | | | 9 | | | | 2 |
| 21 | 23 | 24 | 25 | 7 | 5 | 3 | 1 | 30 |
| | | | | 26 | | | | 32 |
| | | | | 27 | | | | 34 |
| | | | | 28 | | | | 36 |
| | | | | 29 | 31 | 33 | 35 | |
| | | | | | | | | |
| | | | | | | | | |
| | | | | | | | | 38 |
| | | | | | | | 37 | |

Right-Handed

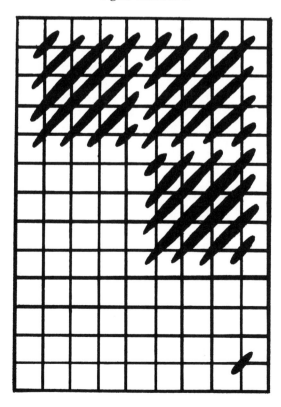

| UP Through | | DOWN Through |
|---|---|---|
| 1 | ———— | 2 |
| 3 | ———— | 4 |
| 5 | ———— | 6 |
| 7 | ———— | 8 |
| 9 | ———— | 10 |
| 11 | ———— | 12 |
| 13 | ———— | 14 |
| 15 | ———— | 16 |
| 17 | ———— | 18 |
| 19 | ———— | 20 |
| 21 | ———— | 22 |
| 23 | ———— | 13 |
| 24 | ———— | 11 |
| 25 | ———— | 9 |
| 26 | ———— | 5 |
| 27 | ———— | 3 |
| 28 | ———— | 1 |
| 29 | ———— | 30 |
| 31 | ———— | 32 |
| 33 | ———— | 34 |
| 35 | ———— | 36 |
| 37 | ———— | 38 |

**Byzantine and Scotch.** 48 rows down, commencing with the Scotch Stitch alternating with the Byzantine. 7 diagonal rows of each. ( see Diagram 4 for Basketweave and Diagram 22 for French knots used for Ladybug in Figure 5).

Diagram 17

| 6 | 8 | 10 | 22 | 20 | 18 | 16 | 14 | 12 | 61 | 63 | 65 | 77 | 75 | 73 | 71 | 69 | 67 | | |
|---|---|---|---|---|---|---|---|---|---|---|---|---|---|---|---|---|---|---|---|
| 4 | | | 9 | | | | | | 11 | | | 64 | | | | | | | 66 |
| 2 | | | 7 | | | | | | 13 | | | 62 | | | | | | | 68 |
| 29 | 1 | 3 | 5 | | | 21 | 19 | 17 | 15 | 58 | 59 | 60 | | | 76 | 74 | 72 | 70 | |
| 31 | | | | | | 23 | | | 57 | | | | | | 78 | | | | |
| 33 | | | | | | 24 | | | 56 | | | | | | 79 | | | | |
| 35 | | 28 | 27 | 26 | 25 | 53 | 54 | 55 | | | 83 | 82 | 81 | 80 | | | | | |
| 37 | | | 30 | | | 52 | | | | | 84 | | | | | | | | |
| 39 | | | 32 | | | 51 | | | | | 85 | | | | | | | | |
| 45 | 38 | 36 | 34 | 48 | 49 | 50 | | | 89 | 88 | 87 | 86 | | | | | | | |
| 43 | | | 47 | | | | | | 90 | | | | | | | | | | |
| 41 | | | 46 | | | | | | 91 | | | | | | | | | | |
| 102 | 40 | 42 | 44 | | | 95 | 94 | 93 | 92 | | | | | | | | | | |
| 104 | | | | | | 96 | | | | | | | | | | | | | |
| 106 | | | | | | 97 | | | | | | | | | | | | | |
| 108 | | | 101 | 100 | 99 | 98 | | | | | | | | | | | | | |
| 110 | | | 103 | | | | | | | | | | | | | | | | |
| 112 | | | 105 | | | | | | | | | | | | | | | | |
| | 111 | 109 | 107 | | | | | | | | | | | | | | | | |
| | | | | | | | | | | | | | | | | | | | |
| | | | | | | | | | | | | | | | | | | | |
| | 113 | | | | | | | | | | | | | | | | | | |

Left-Handed

| UP Through | DOWN Through |
|---|---|
| 1 | 2 |
| 3 | 4 |
| 5 | 6 |
| 7 | 8 |
| 9 | 10 |
| 11 | 12 |
| 13 | 14 |
| 15 | 16 |
| 17 | 18 |
| 19 | 20 |
| 21 | 22 |
| 23 | 9 |
| 24 | 7 |
| 25 | 5 |
| 26 | 3 |
| 27 | 1 |
| 28 | 29 |
| 30 | 31 |
| 32 | 33 |
| 34 | 35 |
| 36 | 37 |
| 38 | 39 |
| 40 | 41 |
| 42 | 43 |
| 44 | 45 |
| 46 | 38 |
| 47 | 36 |
| 48 | 32 |
| 49 | 30 |
| 50 | 28 |
| 51 | 27 |
| 52 | 26 |
| 53 | 24 |
| 54 | 23 |
| 55 | 21 |
| 56 | 19 |
| 57 | 17 |
| 58 | 13 |
| 59 | 11 |

| UP Through | | DOWN Through |
|---|---|---|
| 60 | ———————— | 61 |
| 62 | ———————— | 63 |
| 64 | ———————— | 65 |
| 66 | ———————— | 67 |
| 68 | ———————— | 69 |
| 70 | ———————— | 71 |
| 72 | ———————— | 73 |
| 74 | ———————— | 75 |
| 76 | ———————— | 77 |
| 78 | ———————— | 64 |
| 79 | ———————— | 62 |
| 80 | ———————— | 60 |
| 81 | ———————— | 59 |
| 82 | ———————— | 58 |
| 83 | ———————— | 15 |
| 84 | ———————— | 57 |
| 85 | ———————— | 56 |
| 86 | ———————— | 55 |
| 87 | ———————— | 54 |
| 88 | ———————— | 53 |
| 89 | ———————— | 25 |
| 90 | ———————— | 52 |
| 91 | ———————— | 51 |
| 92 | ———————— | 50 |
| 93 | ———————— | 49 |
| 94 | ———————— | 48 |
| 95 | ———————— | 34 |
| 96 | ———————— | 47 |
| 97 | ———————— | 46 |
| 98 | ———————— | 44 |
| 99 | ———————— | 42 |
| 100 | ———————— | 40 |
| 101 | ———————— | 102 |
| 103 | ———————— | 104 |
| 105 | ———————— | 106 |
| 107 | ———————— | 108 |
| 109 | ———————— | 110 |
| 111 | ———————— | 112 |
| 113 | | |

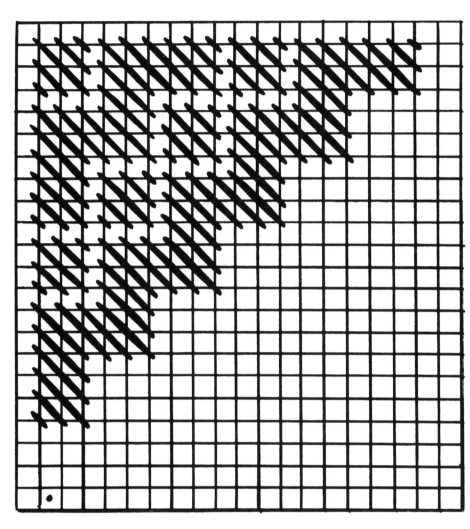

Left-Handed

*(see pages 58 and 59 for Right-Handed Diagrams)*

Figure 5

Left-Handed

***Byzantine and Scotch.*** 48 rows down, commencing with the Scotch Stitch alternating with the Byzantine. 7 diagonal rows of each. (see Diagram 4 for Basketweave and Diagram 22 for French knots used for Ladybug in Figure 5).

Diagram 17

| | | 67 | 69 | 71 | 73 | 75 | 77 | 65 | 63 | 61 | 12 | 14 | 16 | 18 | 20 | 22 | 10 | 8 | 6 |
|---|---|---|---|---|---|---|---|---|---|---|---|---|---|---|---|---|---|---|---|
| | 66 | | | | | | 64 | | | 11 | | | | | | 9 | | | 4 |
| | 68 | | | | | | 62 | | | 13 | | | | | | 7 | | | 2 |
| | 70 | 72 | 74 | 76 | | | 60 | 59 | 58 | 15 | 17 | 19 | 21 | | | 5 | 3 | 1 | 29 |
| | | | | 78 | | | | | | 57 | | | 23 | | | | | | 31 |
| | | | | 79 | | | | | | 56 | | | 24 | | | | | | 33 |
| | | | | 80 | 81 | 82 | 83 | | | 55 | 54 | 53 | 25 | 26 | 27 | 28 | | | 35 |
| | | | | | | | 84 | | | | | | 52 | | | 30 | | | 37 |
| | | | | | | | 85 | | | | | | 51 | | | 32 | | | 39 |
| | | | | | 86 | 87 | 88 | 89 | | | | | 50 | 49 | 48 | 34 | 36 | 38 | 45 |
| | | | | | | | | 90 | | | | | | | | 47 | | | 43 |
| | | | | | | | | 91 | | | | | | | | 46 | | | 41 |
| | | | | | | | | 92 | 93 | 94 | 95 | | | | | 44 | 42 | 40 | 102 |
| | | | | | | | | | | | 96 | | | | | | | | 104 |
| | | | | | | | | | | | 97 | | | | | | | | 106 |
| | | | | | | | | | | | 98 | 99 | 100 | 101 | | | | | 108 |
| | | | | | | | | | | | | | | 103 | | | | | 110 |
| | | | | | | | | | | | | | | 106 | | | | | 112 |
| | | | | | | | | | | | | | | 107 | 109 | 111 | | | |
| | | | | | | | | | | | | | | | | | | | |
| | | | | | | | | | | | | | | | | | | | |
| | | | | | | | | | | | | | | | 113 | | | | |

Right-Handed

| UP Through | DOWN Through |
|---|---|
| 1 | 2 |
| 3 | 4 |
| 5 | 6 |
| 7 | 8 |
| 9 | 10 |
| 11 | 12 |
| 13 | 14 |
| 15 | 16 |
| 17 | 18 |
| 19 | 20 |
| 21 | 22 |
| 23 | 9 |
| 24 | 7 |
| 25 | 5 |
| 26 | 3 |
| 27 | 1 |
| 28 | 29 |
| 30 | 31 |
| 32 | 33 |
| 34 | 35 |
| 36 | 37 |
| 38 | 39 |
| 40 | 41 |
| 42 | 43 |
| 44 | 45 |
| 46 | 38 |
| 47 | 36 |
| 48 | 32 |
| 49 | 30 |
| 50 | 28 |
| 51 | 27 |
| 52 | 26 |
| 53 | 24 |
| 54 | 23 |
| 55 | 21 |
| 56 | 19 |
| 57 | 17 |
| 58 | 13 |
| 59 | 11 |

| UP Through | DOWN Through |
|---|---|
| 60 —————— 61 |
| 62 —————— 63 |
| 64 —————— 65 |
| 66 —————— 67 |
| 68 —————— 69 |
| 70 —————— 71 |
| 72 —————— 73 |
| 74 —————— 75 |
| 76 —————— 77 |
| 78 —————— 64 |
| 79 —————— 62 |
| 80 —————— 60 |
| 81 —————— 59 |
| 82 —————— 58 |
| 83 —————— 15 |
| 84 —————— 57 |
| 85 —————— 56 |
| 86 —————— 55 |
| 87 —————— 54 |
| 88 —————— 53 |
| 89 —————— 25 |
| 90 —————— 52 |
| 91 —————— 51 |
| 92 —————— 50 |
| 93 —————— 49 |
| 94 —————— 48 |
| 95 —————— 34 |
| 96 —————— 47 |
| 97 —————— 46 |
| 98 —————— 44 |
| 99 —————— 42 |
| 100 —————— 40 |
| 101 —————— 102 |
| 103 —————— 104 |
| 105 —————— 106 |
| 107 —————— 108 |
| 109 —————— 110 |
| 111 —————— 112 |
| 113 |

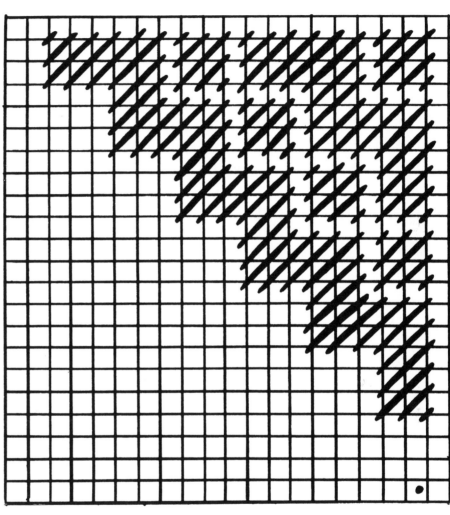

Right-Handed

Figure 5

Right-Handed

**Checkerboard of Basketweave and Counter Direction Scotch.** Worked with 2 threads, alternating units of Basketweave and Counter Direction Scotch. 12 units down, 3 units across. Done in separate colors, you have pattern on pattern on color. Done in a solid color, it gives a smooth, subtle texture.

Diagram 18

| 2 | 6 | 8 | 17 | | 24 | 25 | 26 | 27 | 82 | 84 | 91 | | 98 | 99 | 100 | 101 |
|---|---|---|----|--|----|----|----|----|----|----|----|--|----|----|-----|-----|
| 4 | 1 | 5 | 7 | 16 | | | | 29 | 79 | 81 | 83 | 90 | | | | 103 |
| 11 | 3 | 9 | 15 | 18 | | | | 31 | 80 | 85 | 89 | 92 | | | | 105 |
| 13 | 10 | 14 | 19 | 22 | | | | 33 | 86 | 88 | 93 | 96 | | | | 107 |
| | 12 | 20 | 21 | 23 | 28 | 30 | 32 | | 87 | 94 | 95 | 97 | 102 | 104 | 106 | |
| 34 | | | 39 | 63 | 65 | 66 | 72 | | | | 109 | | | | | |
| 35 | | | 41 | 64 | 67 | 71 | 73 | | | | 111 | | | | | |
| 36 | | | 43 | 68 | 70 | 74 | 77 | | | | 113 | | | | | |
| 37 | 38 | 40 | 42 | | 69 | 75 | 76 | 78 | 108 | 110 | 112 | | | | | |
| 46 | 44 | 47 | 48 | 56 | | | 115 | | | | | | | | | |
| 51 | 45 | 49 | 55 | 57 | | | 117 | | | | | | | | | |
| 53 | 50 | 54 | 58 | 61 | | | 119 | | | | | | | | | |
| | 52 | 59 | 60 | 62 | 114 | 116 | 118 | | | | | | | | | |
| 100 | | | 125 | | | | | | | | | | | | | |
| 121 | | | 127 | | | | | | | | | | | | | |
| 122 | | | 129 | | | | | | | | | | | | | |
| 123 | 124 | 126 | 128 | | | | | | | | | | | | | |
| | 130 | | | | | | | | | | | | | | | |

Left-Handed *(see pages 62 and 63 for Right-Handed Diagrams)*

| UP Through | DOWN Throu |
|---|---|
| 1 | 2 |
| 3 | 4 |
| 5 | 6 |
| 7 | 8 |
| 9 | 1 |
| 10 | 11 |
| 12 | 13 |
| 14 | 3 |
| 15 | 5 |
| 16 | 17 |
| 18 | 7 |
| 19 | 9 |
| 20 | 10 |
| 21 | 14 |
| 22 | 15 |
| 23 | 19 |
| 16 | 24 |
| 18 | 25 |
| 22 | 26 |
| 23 | 27 |
| 28 | 29 |
| 30 | 31 |
| 32 | 33 |
| 34 | 12 |
| 35 | 20 |
| 36 | 21 |
| 37 | 23 |
| 38 | 39 |
| 40 | 41 |
| 42 | 43 |
| 44 | 37 |
| 45 | 46 |
| 47 | 38 |
| 48 | 40 |
| 49 | 44 |
| 50 | 51 |
| 52 | 53 |
| 54 | 45 |
| 55 | 47 |
| 56 | 42 |
| 57 | 48 |
| 58 | 49 |
| 59 | 50 |
| 60 | 54 |
| 61 | 55 |
| 62 | 58 |
| 63 | 23 |
| 64 | 39 |
| 65 | 28 |
| 66 | 30 |
| 67 | 63 |
| 68 | 41 |
| 69 | 43 |

| UP Through | DOWN Through |
|---|---|
| 70 ————————— 64 |
| 71 ————————— 65 |
| 72 ————————— 32 |
| 73 ————————— 66 |
| 74 ————————— 67 |
| 75 ————————— 68 |
| 76 ————————— 70 |
| 77 ————————— 71 |
| 78 ————————— 74 |
| 79 ————————— 27 |
| 80 ————————— 29 |
| 81 ————————— 82 |
| 83 ————————— 84 |
| 85 ————————— 79 |
| 86 ————————— 31 |
| 87 ————————— 33 |
| 88 ————————— 80 |
| 89 ————————— 81 |
| 90 ————————— 91 |
| 92 ————————— 83 |
| 93 ————————— 85 |
| 94 ————————— 86 |
| 95 ————————— 88 |
| 96 ————————— 89 |
| 97 ————————— 93 |
| 90 ————————— 98 |
| 92 ————————— 99 |
| 96 ————————— 100 |
| 97 ————————— 101 |
| 102 ————————— 103 |
| 104 ————————— 105 |
| 106 ————————— 107 |
| 72 ————————— 87 |
| 73 ————————— 94 |
| 77 ————————— 95 |
| 78 ————————— 97 |
| 108 ————————— 109 |
| 110 ————————— 111 |
| 112 ————————— 113 |
| 56 ————————— 69 |
| 57 ————————— 75 |
| 61 ————————— 76 |
| 62 ————————— 78 |
| 114 ————————— 115 |
| 116 ————————— 117 |
| 118 ————————— 119 |
| 100 ————————— 52 |
| 121 ————————— 59 |
| 122 ————————— 60 |
| 123 ————————— 62 |
| 124 ————————— 125 |
| 126 ————————— 127 |
| 128 ————————— 129 |
| 130 |

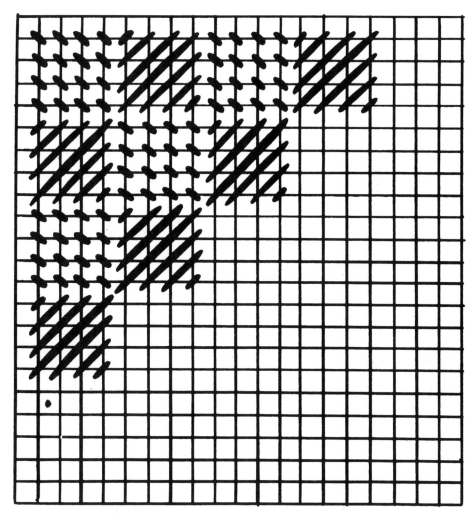

Diagram 18

Left-Handed

***Checkerboard of Basketweave and Counter Direction Scotch.*** Worked with 2 threads, alternating units of Basketweave and Counter Direction Scotch. 12 units down, 3 units across. Done in separate colors, you have pattern on pattern on color. Done in a solid color, it gives a smooth, subtle texture.

Diagram 18

| | | 101 | 100 | 99 | 98 | | 91 | 84 | 82 | 27 | 26 | 25 | 24 | | 17 | 8 | 6 | 2 |
|---|---|---|---|---|---|---|---|---|---|---|---|---|---|---|---|---|---|---|
| | | 103 | | | | 90 | 83 | 81 | 79 | 29 | | | 16 | 7 | 5 | 1 | 4 |
| | | 105 | | | | 92 | 89 | 85 | 80 | 31 | | | 18 | 15 | 9 | 3 | 11 |
| | | 107 | | | | 96 | 93 | 88 | 86 | 33 | | | 22 | 19 | 14 | 10 | 13 |
| | | | 106 | 104 | 102 | 97 | 95 | 94 | 87 | | 32 | 30 | 28 | 23 | 21 | 20 | 12 |
| | | | | | | 109 | | | | 72 | 66 | 65 | 63 | 39 | | | 34 |
| | | | | | | 111 | | | | 73 | 71 | 67 | 64 | 41 | | | 35 |
| | | | | | | 113 | | | | 77 | 74 | 70 | 68 | 43 | | | 36 |
| | | | | | 112 | 110 | 108 | 78 | 76 | 75 | 69 | | 42 | 40 | 38 | 37 |
| | | | | | | | 115 | | | 56 | 48 | 47 | 44 | 46 |
| | | | | | | | 117 | | | 57 | 55 | 49 | 45 | 51 |
| | | | | | | | 119 | | | 61 | 58 | 54 | 50 | 53 |
| | | | | | | 118 | 116 | 114 | 62 | 60 | 59 | 52 | |
| | | | | | | | | | 125 | | | 100 |
| | | | | | | | | | 127 | | | 121 |
| | | | | | | | | | 129 | | | 122 |
| | | | | | | | | 128 | 126 | 124 | 123 |
| | | | | | | | | | | 130 |

Right-Handed

| UP Through | DOWN Through |
|---|---|
| 1 | 2 |
| 3 | 4 |
| 5 | 6 |
| 7 | 8 |
| 9 | 1 |
| 10 | 11 |
| 12 | 13 |
| 14 | 3 |
| 15 | 5 |
| 16 | 17 |
| 18 | 7 |
| 19 | 9 |
| 20 | 10 |
| 21 | 14 |
| 22 | 15 |
| 23 | 19 |
| 16 | 24 |
| 18 | 25 |
| 22 | 26 |
| 23 | 27 |
| 28 | 29 |
| 30 | 31 |
| 32 | 33 |
| 34 | 12 |
| 35 | 20 |
| 36 | 21 |
| 37 | 23 |
| 38 | 39 |
| 40 | 41 |
| 42 | 43 |
| 44 | 37 |
| 45 | 46 |
| 47 | 38 |
| 48 | 40 |
| 49 | 44 |
| 50 | 51 |
| 52 | 53 |
| 54 | 45 |
| 55 | 47 |
| 56 | 42 |
| 57 | 48 |
| 58 | 49 |
| 59 | 50 |
| 60 | 54 |
| 61 | 55 |
| 62 | 58 |
| 63 | 23 |
| 64 | 39 |
| 65 | 28 |
| 66 | 30 |
| 67 | 63 |
| 68 | 41 |
| 69 | 43 |

| UP Through | DOWN Through |
|---|---|
| 70 | 64 |
| 71 | 65 |
| 72 | 32 |
| 73 | 66 |
| 74 | 67 |
| 75 | 68 |
| 76 | 70 |
| 77 | 71 |
| 78 | 74 |
| 79 | 27 |
| 80 | 29 |
| 81 | 82 |
| 83 | 84 |
| 85 | 79 |
| 86 | 31 |
| 87 | 33 |
| 88 | 80 |
| 89 | 81 |
| 90 | 91 |
| 92 | 83 |
| 93 | 85 |
| 94 | 86 |
| 95 | 88 |
| 96 | 89 |
| 97 | 93 |
| 90 | 98 |
| 92 | 99 |
| 96 | 100 |
| 97 | 101 |
| 102 | 103 |
| 104 | 105 |
| 106 | 107 |
| 72 | 87 |
| 73 | 94 |
| 77 | 95 |
| 78 | 97 |
| 108 | 109 |
| 110 | 111 |
| 112 | 113 |
| 56 | 69 |
| 57 | 75 |
| 61 | 76 |
| 62 | 78 |
| 114 | 115 |
| 116 | 117 |
| 118 | 119 |
| 100 | 52 |
| 121 | 59 |
| 122 | 60 |
| 123 | 62 |
| 124 | 125 |
| 126 | 127 |
| 128 | 129 |
| 130 | |

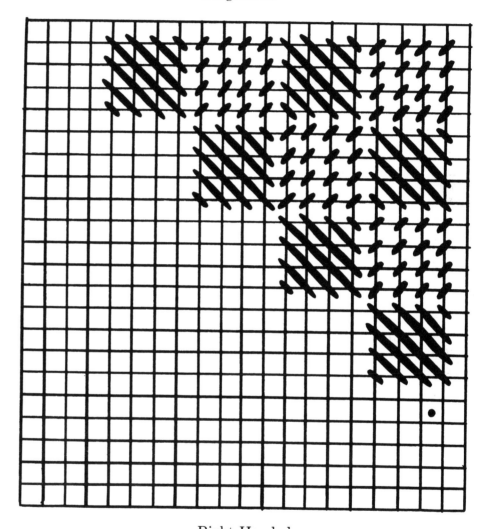

Diagram 18

Right-Handed

*Bargello.* Worked with 1 strand. 48 rows down, 40 rows across. Flowing and simple. This stitch can give the illusion of sea, grass, or sky in subtly graded colors.

Diagram 19

| UP Through | | DOWN Through |
|---|---|---|
| 1 | ———————— | 2 |
| 3 | ———————— | 4 |
| 5 | ———————— | 6 |
| 7 | ———————— | 8 |
| 9 | ———————— | 10 |
| 11 | ———————— | 12 |
| 13 | ———————— | 14 |
| 15 | ———————— | 16 |
| 17 | ———————— | 18 |
| 19 | ———————— | 17 |
| 20 | ———————— | 15 |
| 21 | ———————— | 13 |
| 22 | ———————— | 11 |
| 23 | ———————— | 9 |
| 24 | ———————— | 7 |
| 25 | ———————— | 5 |
| 26 | ———————— | 3 |
| 27 | ———————— | 1 |
| 28 | ———————— | 27 |
| 29 | ———————— | 26 |

Left-Handed

**Bargello.** Worked with 1 strand. 48 rows down, 40 rows across. Flowing and simple. This stitch can give the illusion of sea, grass, or sky in subtly graded colors.

Diagram 19

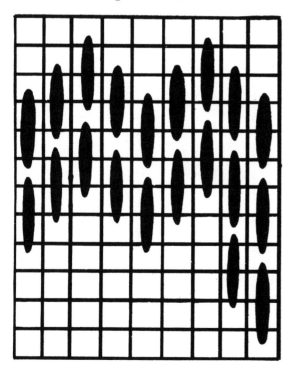

Right-Handed

| UP Through | DOWN Through |
|---|---|
| 1 ————— | 2 |
| 3 ————— | 4 |
| 5 ————— | 6 |
| 7 ————— | 8 |
| 9 ————— | 10 |
| 11 ————— | 12 |
| 13 ————— | 14 |
| 15 ————— | 16 |
| 17 ————— | 18 |
| 19 ————— | 17 |
| 20 ————— | 15 |
| 21 ————— | 13 |
| 22 ————— | 11 |
| 23 ————— | 9 |
| 24 ————— | 7 |
| 25 ————— | 5 |
| 26 ————— | 3 |
| 27 ————— | 1 |
| 28 ————— | 27 |
| 29 ————— | 26 |

***Surrey Stitch—Tufted.*** Worked with 2 threads, clipped and trimmed. Surrey Stitch is used for body of bee in, Figure 6). Here is a difficult stitch which is marvelous for forming raised areas. Bumblebee wings in Basketweave (see Diagram 4).

Diagram 20

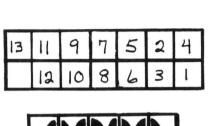

The Surrey Stitch should be worked from the bottom of the canvas up. This allows for clear vision while keeping the loops out of the way. After all the loops are completed, they can be clipped and trimmed to form the tufting.

| UP Through | | DOWN Through | |
|---|---|---|---|
| 1 | ——————— | 2 | makes a loop |
| 3 | ——————— | 4 | |
| 3 | ——————— | 5 | makes a loop |
| 6 | ——————— | 2 | |
| 6 | ——————— | 7 | makes a loop |
| 8 | ——————— | 5 | |
| 8 | ——————— | 9 | makes a loop |
| 10 | ——————— | 7 | |
| 10 | ——————— | 11 | makes a loop |
| 12 | ——————— | 9 | |
| 12 | ——————— | 13 | makes a loop |

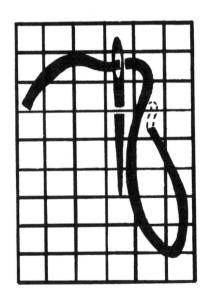

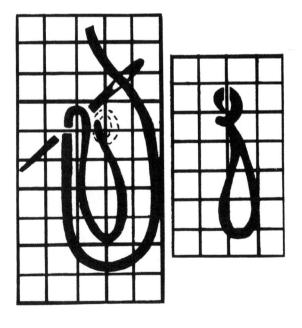

Figure 6
Left-Handed

Left-Handed

***Surrey Stitch—Tufted.*** Worked with 2 threads, clipped and trimmed. Surrey Stitch is used for body of bee in, Figure 6). Here is a difficult stitch which is marvelous for forming raised areas. Bumblebee wings in Basketweave (see Diagram 4).

Diagram 20

The Surrey Stitch should be worked from the bottom of the canvas up. This allows for clear vision while keeping the loops out of the way. After all the loops are completed, they can be clipped and trimmed to form the tufting.

| UP Through | | DOWN Through | |
|---|---|---|---|
| 1 | ———————— | 2 | makes a loop |
| 3 | ———————— | 4 | |
| 3 | ———————— | 5 | makes a loop |
| 6 | ———————— | 2 | |
| 6 | ———————— | 7 | makes a loop |
| 8 | ———————— | 5 | |
| 8 | ———————— | 9 | makes a loop |
| 10 | ———————— | 7 | |
| 10 | ———————— | 11 | makes a loop |
| 12 | ———————— | 9 | |
| 12 | ———————— | 13 | makes a loop |

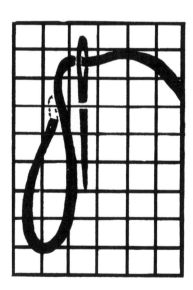

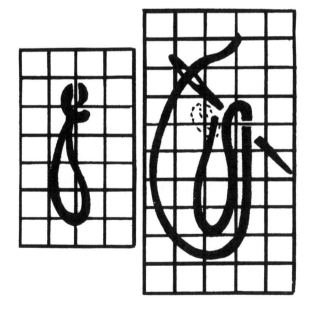

Right-Handed

Figure 6

Right-Handed

*Interlocking Gobelin.* Worked in 2 threads. On flower petals (see Figure 7). This is the Slanting Gobelin Stitch, but it doubles back on the stitch above, being worked every row, instead of every other row as in the Slanting Gobelin. It somehow has a knitted look to me.

Diagram 21

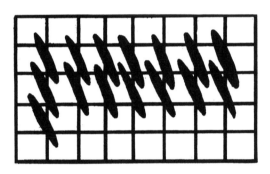

Left-Handed

| UP Through | | DOWN Through |
|---|---|---|
| 1 | ———————— | 2 |
| 3 | ———————— | 4 |
| 5 | ———————— | 6 |
| 7 | ———————— | 8 |
| 9 | ———————— | 10 |
| 11 | ———————— | 12 |
| 13 | ———————— | 14 |
| 15 | ———————— | 16 |
| 17 | ———————— | 18 |
| 19 | ———————— | 20 |
| 21 | ———————— | 22 |
| 23 | ———————— | 24 |
| 25 | ———————— | 26 |
| 27 | ———————— | 28 |
| 29 | ———————— | 30 |

Figure 7

Left-Handed

***Interlocking Gobelin.*** Worked in 2 threads. On flower petals (see Figure 7). This is the Slanting Gobelin Stitch, but it doubles back on the stitch above, being worked every row, instead of every other row as in the Slanting Gobelin. It somehow has a knitted look to me.

Diagram 21

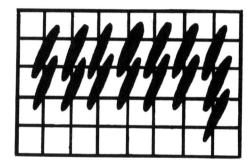

Right-Handed

| UP Through | DOWN Through |
|---|---|
| 1 ——————— | 2 |
| 3 ——————— | 4 |
| 5 ——————— | 6 |
| 7 ——————— | 8 |
| 9 ——————— | 10 |
| 11 ——————— | 12 |
| 13 ——————— | 14 |
| 15 ——————— | 16 |
| 17 ——————— | 18 |
| 19 ——————— | 20 |
| 21 ——————— | 22 |
| 23 ——————— | 24 |
| 25 ——————— | 26 |
| 27 ——————— | 28 |
| 29 ——————— | 30 |

Figure 7

Right-Handed

*French Knots.* Worked with 2 threads. On center of flower (see Figure 7). This is really an embroidery stitch, but then so many of the needlepoint stitches are, they have been adapted to the needlepoint canvas. These knots as shown here give the center of the flower, and the antennae on the butterfly and bee the finishing touches. They also make the spots stand out on the ladybug.

Diagram 22

| | | | | | | | |
|---|---|---|---|---|---|---|---|
| 2 | 4 | 6 | 8 | | | | |
| 10 | 1 | 3 | 5 | 7 | | | |
| | 9 | 11 | 12 | 13 | | | |

Left-Handed

| UP Through | DOWN Through |
|---|---|
| 1 ——————— | 2 |
| 3 ——————— | 4 |
| 5 ——————— | 6 |
| 7 ——————— | 8 |
| 9 ——————— | 10 |
| 11 ——————— | 1 |
| 12 ——————— | 3 |
| 13 ——————— | 5 |

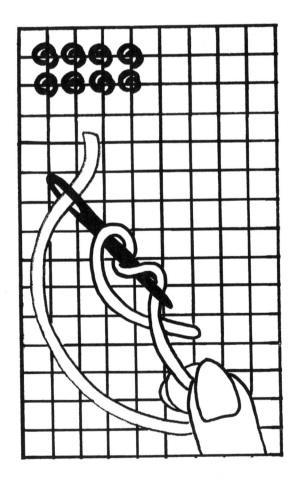

***French Knots.*** Worked with 2 threads. On center of flower (see Figure 7). This is really an embroidery stitch, but then so many of the needlepoint stitches are, they have been adapted to the needlepoint canvas. These knots as shown here give the center of the flower, and the antennae on the butterfly and bee the finishing touches. They also make the spots stand out on the ladybug.

Diagram 22

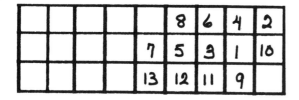

Right-Handed

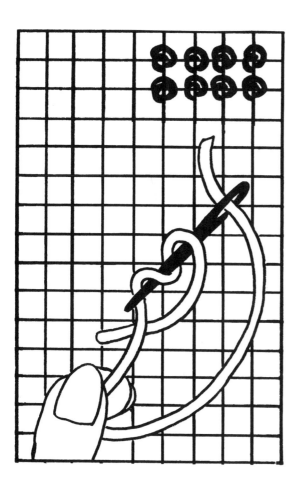

| UP Through | | DOWN Through |
|---|---|---|
| 1 | ———————— | 2 |
| 3 | ———————— | 4 |
| 5 | ———————— | 6 |
| 7 | ———————— | 8 |
| 9 | ———————— | 10 |
| 11 | ———————— | 1 |
| 12 | ———————— | 3 |
| 13 | ———————— | 5 |

***Satin Stitch.*** Worked with 1 strand on stem of flower (see Figure 7). Another embroidery stitch that is ideal for stems, as shown here.

Diagram 23

|  | UP Through | DOWN Through |
|---|---|---|
|  | 1 ———————— | 2 |
|  | 3 ———————— | 4 |
|  | 5 ———————— | 6 |
|  | 7 ———————— | 8 |
|  | 9 ———————— | 10 |
|  | 11 ———————— | 12 |
|  | 13 ———————— | 14 |
|  | 15 |  |

Left-Handed

Right-Handed

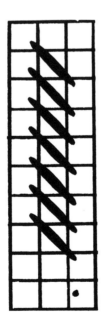

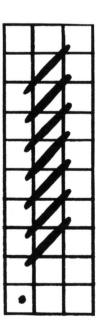

**Leaf Stitch.** Worked with 2 threads. For leaves on flower. 4 units for each leaf (see Figure 7). This is without a doubt one of the most difficult stitches. If you have the patience to do it, it is worth it. It seemed appropriate to use it here on the leaves of the daisy.

Diagram 24

Left-Handed

*(see page 74 for Right-Handed Diagram)*

Starting in the left-hand corner:

| UP Through | DOWN Through |
|---|---|
| 11 ————— | 12 |
| 9 ————— | 13 |
| 7 ————— | 14 |
| 5 ————— | 6 |
| 3 ————— | 4 |
| 1 ————— | 2 |

Left-handers move 3 holes to the right and 4 holes down.

| UP Through | DOWN Through |
|---|---|
| 1*————— | 2* |
| 3 ————— | 4 |
| 5 ————— | 6 |
| 7 ————— | 8 |
| 9 ————— | 10 |
| 11 ————— | 12 |
| 9 ————— | 13 |
| 7 ————— | 14 |
| 5 ————— | 15 |
| 3 ————— | 16 |
| 1 ————— | 17 |

Left-handers move 6 holes to the left and 11 holes down. Start with pattern at * to form next leaf.

| 12 | | | | | 12 | | | | |
|---|---|---|---|---|---|---|---|---|---|
| | | | | | | | | | |
| | 13 | | | 10 | | 13 | | | |
| | | 14 | 8 | | | | 14 | | |
| 11 | | | 6 | | | | | | 15 |
| | | | 4 | | | | | | 16 |
| 9 | | | 2 | | 9 | | | | 17 |
| 7 | | | 12 | | 7 | | | | 12 |
| 5 | | | | | 5 | | | | |
| 3 | 10 | | 13 | | 3 | 10 | | | |
| 1 | 8 | | | 14 | 1 | 8 | | | |
| 6 | | 11 | | | 15 | | 11 | | |
| 4 | | | | | 16 | | | | |
| 2 | | 9 | | | 17 | | 9 | | |
| | | 7 | | | | | 7 | | |
| | | 5 | | | | | 5 | | |
| | | 3 | | | | | 3 | | |
| | | 1 | | | | | 1 | | |

*Leaf Stitch.* Worked with 2 threads. For leaves on flower. 4 units for each leaf (see Figure 7). This is without a doubt one of the most difficult stitches. If you have the patience to do it, it is worth it. It seemed appropriate to use it here on the leaves of the daisy.

Diagram 24

Right-Handed

Starting in the right-hand corner:

| UP Through | DOWN Through |
|---|---|
| 11 ——————— | 12 |
| 9 ——————— | 13 |
| 7 ——————— | 14 |
| 5 ——————— | 6 |
| 3 ——————— | 4 |
| 1 ——————— | 2 |

Right-handers move 3 holes to the left and 4 holes down.

| UP Through | DOWN Through |
|---|---|
| 1* ——————— | 2* |
| 3 ——————— | 4 |
| 5 ——————— | 6 |
| 7 ——————— | 8 |
| 9 ——————— | 10 |
| 11 ——————— | 12 |
| 9 ——————— | 13 |
| 7 ——————— | 14 |
| 5 ——————— | 15 |
| 3 ——————— | 16 |
| 1 ——————— | 17 |

Right-handers move 6 holes to the right and 11 holes down. Start with pattern at * to form next leaf.

***Old Florentine Stitch.*** Worked with 1 strand. 86 rows across (or 21 units). 48 rows down (or 7½ units). The Old Florentine Stitch forms a handsome and bold pattern. It needs space to be shown off at its best. Being worked over several threads it cannot withstand harsh treatment, and is easily snagged. Wings of butterfly (Figure 8) done in Strawberry Stitch (Diagram 7). Butterfly body in Surrey Stitch (see Diagram 20).

Diagram 25

Left-Handed

*(see page 76 for*
*Right-Handed Diagram)*

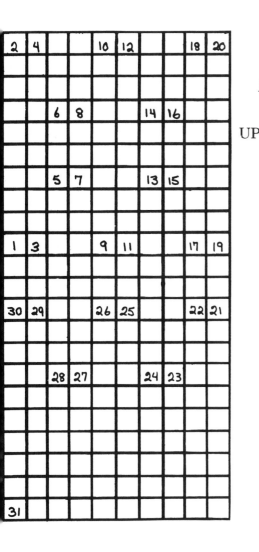

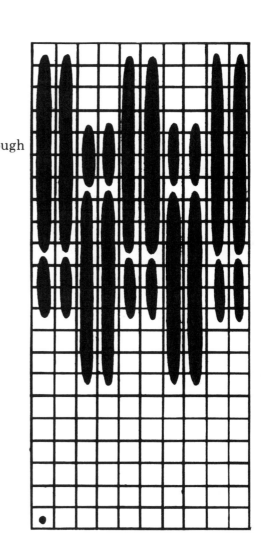

| UP Through | DOWN Through |
|---|---|
| 1 | 2 |
| 3 | 4 |
| 5 | 6 |
| 7 | 8 |
| 9 | 10 |
| 11 | 12 |
| 13 | 14 |
| 15 | 16 |
| 17 | 18 |
| 19 | 20 |
| 21 | 19 |
| 22 | 17 |
| 23 | 15 |
| 24 | 13 |
| 25 | 11 |
| 26 | 9 |
| 27 | 7 |
| 28 | 5 |
| 29 | 3 |
| 30 | 1 |
| 31 | |

Figure 8
Left-Handed

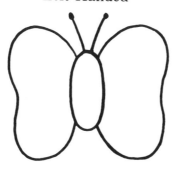

***Old Florentine Stitch.*** Worked with 1 strand. 86 rows across (or 21 units). 48 rows down (or 7½ units). The Old Florentine Stitch forms a handsome and bold pattern. It needs space to be shown off at its best. Being worked over several threads it cannot withstand harsh treatment, and is easily snagged. Wings of butterfly (Figure 8) done in Strawberry Stitch (Diagram 7). Butterfly body in Surrey Stitch (see Diagram 20).

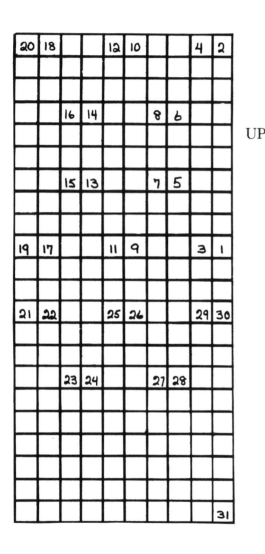

Diagram 25

Right-Handed

| UP Through | | DOWN Through |
|---|---|---|
| 1 | ——————— | 2 |
| 3 | ——————— | 4 |
| 5 | ——————— | 6 |
| 7 | ——————— | 8 |
| 9 | ——————— | 10 |
| 11 | ——————— | 12 |
| 13 | ——————— | 14 |
| 15 | ——————— | 16 |
| 17 | ——————— | 18 |
| 19 | ——————— | 20 |
| 21 | ——————— | 19 |
| 22 | ——————— | 17 |
| 23 | ——————— | 15 |
| 24 | ——————— | 13 |
| 25 | ——————— | 11 |
| 26 | ——————— | 9 |
| 27 | ——————— | 7 |
| 28 | ——————— | 5 |
| 29 | ——————— | 3 |
| 30 | ——————— | 1 |
| 31 | | |

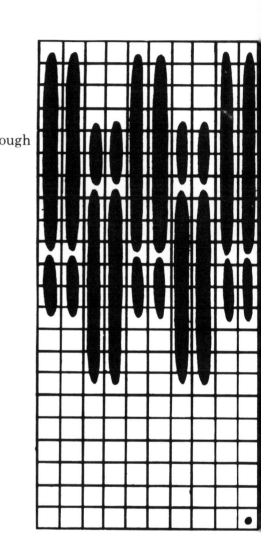

Figure 8

Right-Handed

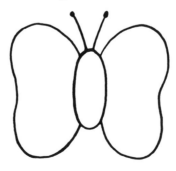

**Slanting Gobelin Stitch.** Worked over 2 rows of canvas with 2 threads. 48 rows down and 25 units across. This is as simple as the regular Gobelin Stitch. If worked over two threads, it will withstand a good deal of wear and tear, so can be used on a rug.

Diagram 26

| UP Through | DOWN Through |
|:---:|:---:|
| 1 ————— | 2 |
| 3 ————— | 4 |
| 5 ————— | 6 |
| 7 ————— | 8 |
| 9 ————— | 10 |
| 11 ————— | 12 |
| 13 ————— | 9 |
| 14 ————— | 7 |
| 15 ————— | 5 |
| 16 ————— | 3 |
| 17 ————— | 1 |
| 18 ————— | 19 |
| 20 ————— | 21 |

Left-Handed

Right-Handed

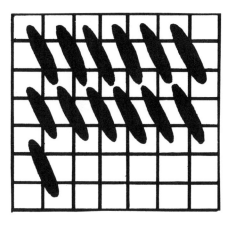

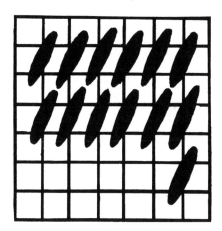

**Slanting Horizontal Gobelin** and **French Knots.** Worked with 2 threads. Diagram 22, shows French Knots worked in units of 4 which interrupt the re-positioned Gobelin stitches.

Diagram 27

Left-Handed

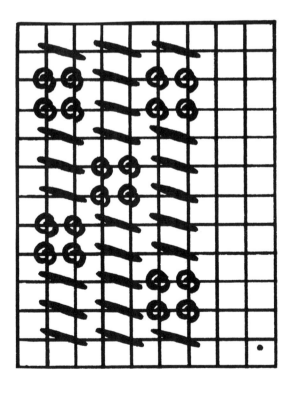

| UP Through | | DOWN Through |
|---|---|---|
| | 1 ———————— | 2 |
| | 3 ———————— | 4 |
| Slanting Gobelin | 5 ———————— | 6 |
| sideways. | 7 ———————— | 8 |
| | 9 ———————— | 10 |
| | 11 ———————— | 12 |
| | 13 ———————— | 14 |
| | Start back up | |
| | 15 ———————— | 11 |
| | 16 ———————— | 9 |
| | 17 ———————— | 18 |
| | 19 ———————— | 20 |
| Slanting Gobelin | 21 ———————— | 7 |
| sideways. | 22 ———————— | 23 |
| | 24 ———————— | 25 |
| | 26 ———————— | 1 |
| | 27 ———————— | 28 |
| | Start back down | |
| | 29 ———————— | 30 |
| | 31 ———————— | 24 |
| | 32 ———————— | 22 |
| Slanting Gobelin | 33 ———————— | 34 |
| sideways. | 35 ———————— | 36 |
| | 37 ———————— | 21 |
| | 38 ———————— | 16 |
| | Start back up | |
| | 39 | |

| UP Through | | DOWN Through |
|---|---|---|
| French Knots in | A ———————— | B |
| groups of four. | C ———————— | D |
| | E ———————— | F |
| | G ———————— | H |

This completes one unit.

A

***Slanting Horizontal Gobelin*** and ***French Knots.*** Worked with 2 threads. Diagram 22, shows French Knots worked in units of 4 which interrupt the re-positioned Gobelin stitches.

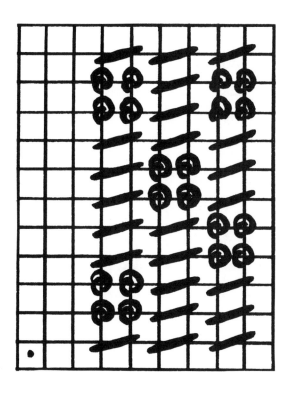

Diagram 27

Right-Handed

| UP Through | | DOWN Through | |
|---|---|---|---|
| 1 | ———————— | 2 | |
| 3 | ———————— | 4 | |
| 5 | ———————— | 6 | Slanting Gobelin |
| 7 | ———————— | 8 | sideways. |
| 9 | ———————— | 10 | |
| 11 | ———————— | 12 | |
| 13 | ———————— | 14 | |
| | Start back up | | |
| 15 | ———————— | 11 | |
| 16 | ———————— | 9 | |
| 17 | ———————— | 18 | |
| 19 | ———————— | 20 | |
| 21 | ———————— | 7 | Slanting Gobelin |
| 22 | ———————— | 23 | sideways. |
| 24 | ———————— | 25 | |
| 26 | ———————— | 1 | |
| 27 | ———————— | 28 | |
| | Start back down | | |
| 29 | ———————— | 30 | |
| 31 | ———————— | 24 | |
| 32 | ———————— | 22 | |
| 33 | ———————— | 34 | Slanting Gobelin |
| 35 | ———————— | 36 | sideways. |
| 37 | ———————— | 21 | |
| 38 | ———————— | 16 | |
| | Start back up | | |
| 39 | | | |

| UP Through | | DOWN Through | |
|---|---|---|---|
| A | ———————— | B | |
| C | ———————— | D | |
| E | ———————— | F | French Knots in |
| G | ———————— | H | groups of four. |
| This completes one unit. | | | |
| A | | | |

***Diagonal Mosaic Stitch.*** Worked with 2 threads. 16 diagonal rows. Unlike the Mosaic, though it has the same name, its pattern is short-long-short-long, etc., instead of short-long-short, etc. If done in alternate colors as shown here, it almost takes on the look of fabric.

Diagram 28

| | | | | | | | | | | | |
|---|---|---|---|---|---|---|---|---|---|---|---|
| 6 | 8 | 10 | 16 | 12 | 14 | 44 | 46 | 48 | | 50 | |
| 2 | | 7 | 9 | | 11 | 13 | | 45 | 47 | | 49 |
| 4 | 1 | 5 | | 17 | 15 | | 42 | 43 | | | 51 |
| 23 | 3 | | 19 | 18 | | 40 | 41 | | | | |
| 25 | | 21 | 20 | | 38 | 39 | | | | | |
| 27 | 24 | 22 | | 36 | 37 | | | | | | |
| 31 | 26 | | 34 | 35 | | | | | | | |
| 29 | | 32 | 33 | | | | | | | | |
| | 28 | 30 | | | | | | | | | |

| UP Through | | DOWN Through |
|---|---|---|
| 1 | ———— | 2 |
| 3 | ———— | 4 |
| 5 | ———— | 6 |
| 7 | ———— | 8 |
| 9 | ———— | 10 |
| 11 | ———— | 12 |
| 13 | ———— | 14 |
| 15 | ———— | 16 |
| 17 | ———— | 9 |
| 18 | ———— | 7 |
| 19 | ———— | 5 |
| 20 | ———— | 1 |
| 21 | ———— | 3 |
| 22 | ———— | 23 |
| 24 | ———— | 25 |
| 26 | ———— | 27 |
| 28 | ———— | 29 |
| 30 | ———— | 31 |
| 32 | ———— | 26 |
| 33 | ———— | 24 |
| 34 | ———— | 22 |
| 35 | ———— | 21 |
| 36 | ———— | 20 |
| 37 | ———— | 19 |
| 38 | ———— | 18 |
| 39 | ———— | 17 |
| 40 | ———— | 15 |
| 41 | ———— | 11 |
| 42 | ———— | 13 |
| 43 | ———— | 44 |
| 45 | ———— | 46 |
| 47 | ———— | 48 |
| 49 | ———— | 50 |
| 51 | | |

Left-Handed

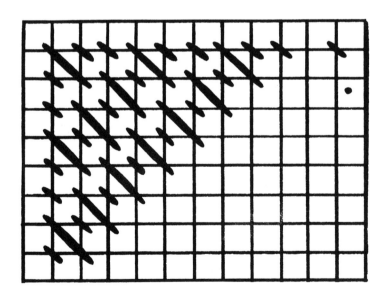

***Diagonal Mosaic Stitch.*** Worked with 2 threads. 16 diagonal rows. Unlike the Mosaic, though it has the same name, its pattern is short-long-short-long, etc., instead of short-long-short, etc. If done in alternate colors as shown here, it almost takes on the look of fabric.

Diagram 28

| | 50 | | 48 | 46 | 44 | 14 | 12 | 16 | 10 | 8 | 6 |
|---|---|---|---|---|---|---|---|---|---|---|---|
| 49 | | 47 | 45 | | 13 | 11 | | 9 | 7 | | 2 |
| 51 | | | 43 | 42 | | 15 | 17 | | 5 | 1 | 4 |
| | | | | 41 | 40 | | 18 | 19 | | 3 | 23 |
| | | | | | 39 | 38 | | 20 | 21 | | 25 |
| | | | | | | 37 | 36 | | 22 | 24 | 27 |
| | | | | | | | 35 | 34 | | 26 | 31 |
| | | | | | | | | 33 | 32 | | 29 |
| | | | | | | | | | 30 | 28 | |

Right-Handed

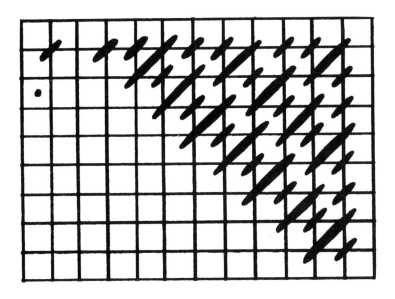

| UP Through | DOWN Through |
|---|---|
| 1 | 2 |
| 3 | 4 |
| 5 | 6 |
| 7 | 8 |
| 9 | 10 |
| 11 | 12 |
| 13 | 14 |
| 15 | 16 |
| 17 | 9 |
| 18 | 7 |
| 19 | 5 |
| 20 | 1 |
| 21 | 3 |
| 22 | 23 |
| 24 | 25 |
| 26 | 27 |
| 28 | 29 |
| 30 | 31 |
| 32 | 26 |
| 33 | 24 |
| 34 | 22 |
| 35 | 21 |
| 36 | 20 |
| 37 | 19 |
| 38 | 18 |
| 39 | 17 |
| 40 | 15 |
| 41 | 11 |
| 42 | 13 |
| 43 | 44 |
| 45 | 46 |
| 47 | 48 |
| 49 | 50 |
| 51 | |

*Upright Knot Stitch.* Worked with 2 threads. 50 rows across. 8 rows down (or 2 units). The long stitch is held down securely by the short Cross Stitch that forms the knot. It stitches up rapidly, and if properly used in small areas, is very distinctive.

Diagram 29

| 2 | 6 | 9 | 12 | 15 | 18 | |
|---|---|---|----|----|----|---|
| | | | | | | |
| 4 | 3 | 7 | 10 | 13 | 16 | 19 |
| | | | | | | |
| 1 | 5 | 8 | 11 | 14 | 17 | |
| | | | | | | |
| 32 | 30 | 28 | 26 | 24 | 21 | 22 |
| | | | | | | |
| 31 | 29 | 27 | 25 | 23 | 20 | |
| | | | | | | |
| 35 | 34 | | | | | |
| | | | | | | |
| 33 | 36 | | | | | |

| UP Through | | DOWN Through |
|---|---|---|
| 1 | ———— | 2 |
| 3 | ———— | 4 |
| 5 | ———— | 6 |
| 7 | ———— | 3 |
| 8 | ———— | 9 |
| 10 | ———— | 7 |
| 11 | ———— | 12 |
| 13 | ———— | 10 |
| 17 | ———— | 18 |
| 19 | ———— | 16 |
| 20 | ———— | 17 |
| 21 | ———— | 22 |
| 23 | ———— | 14 |
| 24 | ———— | 21 |
| 25 | ———— | 11 |
| 26 | ———— | 24 |
| 27 | ———— | 8 |
| 28 | ———— | 26 |
| 29 | ———— | 5 |
| 30 | ———— | 28 |
| 31 | ———— | 1 |
| 32 | ———— | 30 |
| 33 | ———— | 31 |
| 34 | ———— | 35 |
| 36 | | |

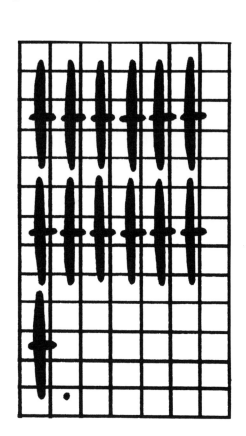

Left-Handed

***Upright Knot Stitch.*** Worked with 2 threads. 50 rows across. 8 rows down (or 2 units). The long stitch is held down securely by the short Cross Stitch that forms the knot. It stitches up rapidly, and if properly used in small areas, is very distinctive.

Diagram 29

| UP Through | | DOWN Through |
|---|---|---|
| 1 | ——————— | 2 |
| 3 | ——————— | 4 |
| 5 | ——————— | 6 |
| 7 | ——————— | 3 |
| 8 | ——————— | 9 |
| 10 | ——————— | 7 |
| 11 | ——————— | 12 |
| 13 | ——————— | 10 |
| 17 | ——————— | 18 |
| 19 | ——————— | 16 |
| 20 | ——————— | 17 |
| 21 | ——————— | 22 |
| 23 | ——————— | 14 |
| 24 | ——————— | 21 |
| 25 | ——————— | 11 |
| 26 | ——————— | 24 |
| 27 | ——————— | 8 |
| 28 | ——————— | 26 |
| 29 | ——————— | 5 |
| 30 | ——————— | 28 |
| 31 | ——————— | 1 |
| 32 | ——————— | 30 |
| 33 | ——————— | 31 |
| 34 | ——————— | 35 |
| 36 | | |

Right-Handed

***Smyrna Cross Stitch.*** Worked with 2 threads. 4 rows down (or 2 units). 25 units across. This is a mini version of the double Leviathan. It is a perky little stitch, and could be used in a border.

Diagram 30

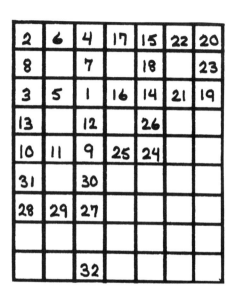

| UP Through | | DOWN Through |
|---|---|---|
| 1 | ———— | 2 |
| 3 | ———— | 4 |
| 5 | ———— | 6 |
| 7 | ———— | 8 |

This completes unit one.

| 9 | ———— | 3 |
| 10 | ———— | 1 |
| 11 | ———— | 5 |
| 12 | ———— | 13 |

This completes unit two.

| 14 | ———— | 4 |
| 1 | ———— | 15 |
| 16 | ———— | 17 |
| 18 | ———— | 4 |

This completes unit three.

| 19 | ———— | 15 |
| 14 | ———— | 20 |
| 21 | ———— | 22 |
| 23 | ———— | 18 |

This completes unit four.

| 24 | ———— | 1 |
| 9 | ———— | 14 |
| 25 | ———— | 16 |
| 26 | ———— | 12 |

This completes unit five.

| 27 | ———— | 10 |
| 28 | ———— | 9 |
| 29 | ———— | 11 |
| 30 | ———— | 31 |

This completes unit six.

| 27 | ———— | 10 |
| 28 | ———— | 9 |
| 29 | ———— | 11 |
| 30 | ———— | 31 |

This completes unit seven.
32

Left-Handed

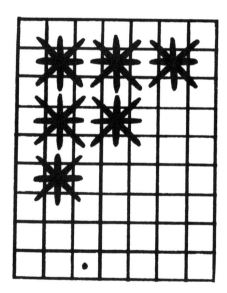

***Smyrna Cross Stitch.*** Worked with 2 threads. 4 rows down (or 2 units). 25 units across. This is a mini version of the double Leviathan. It is a perky little stitch, and could be used in a border.

Diagram 30

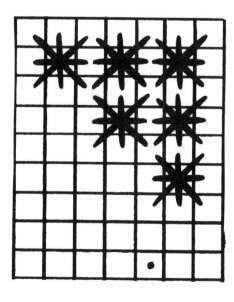

Right-Handed

UP Through      DOWN Through

| UP Through | DOWN Through |
|---|---|
| 1 ————————— | 2 |
| 3 ————————— | 4 |
| 5 ————————— | 6 |
| 7 ————————— | 8 |

This completes unit one.

| | |
|---|---|
| 9 ————————— | 3 |
| 10 ————————— | 1 |
| 11 ————————— | 5 |
| 12 ————————— | 13 |

This completes unit two.

| | |
|---|---|
| 14 ————————— | 4 |
| 1 ————————— | 15 |
| 16 ————————— | 17 |
| 18 ————————— | 4 |

This completes unit three.

| | |
|---|---|
| 19 ————————— | 15 |
| 14 ————————— | 20 |
| 21 ————————— | 22 |
| 23 ————————— | 18 |

This completes unit four.

| | |
|---|---|
| 24 ————————— | 1 |
| 9 ————————— | 14 |
| 25 ————————— | 16 |
| 26 ————————— | 12 |

This completes unit five.

| | |
|---|---|
| 27 ————————— | 10 |
| 28 ————————— | 9 |
| 29 ————————— | 11 |
| 30 ————————— | 31 |

This completes unit six.

| | |
|---|---|
| 27 ————————— | 10 |
| 28 ————————— | 9 |
| 29 ————————— | 11 |
| 30 ————————— | 31 |

This completes unit seven.

32

**Brick Stitch.** Worked with 2 threads. This is probably one of the most popular stitches, and it is certainly one of the easiest. It is excellent for backgrounds, and holds up well.

Diagram 31

| | 2 | | 6 | | 10 | | 14 | |
|---|---|---|---|---|---|---|---|---|
| | | 4 | | 8 | | 12 | | 16 |
| | 1 | | 5 | | 9 | | 13 | |
| | | 3 | | 7 | | 11 | | 15 |
| | 24 | | 22 | | 20 | | 18 | |
| | | 23 | | 21 | | 19 | | 17 |
| | 25 | | | | | | | |

| UP Through | | DOWN Through |
|---|---|---|
| 1 | ———————— | 2 |
| 3 | ———————— | 4 |
| 5 | ———————— | 6 |
| 7 | ———————— | 8 |
| 9 | ———————— | 10 |
| 11 | ———————— | 12 |
| 13 | ———————— | 14 |
| 15 | ———————— | 16 |
| 17 | ———————— | 15 |
| 18 | ———————— | 13 |
| 19 | ———————— | 11 |
| 20 | ———————— | 9 |
| 21 | ———————— | 7 |
| 22 | ———————— | 5 |
| 23 | ———————— | 3 |
| 24 | ———————— | 1 |
| 25 | ———————— | 24 |

Left-Handed

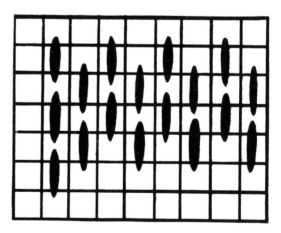

**Brick Stitch.** Worked with 2 threads. This is probably one of the most popular stitches, and it is certainly one of the easiest. It is excellent for backgrounds, and holds up well.

Diagram 31

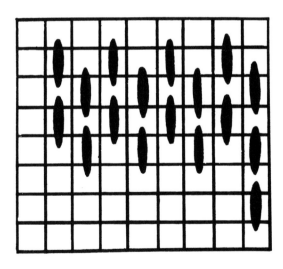

Right-Handed

| UP Through | DOWN Through |
|---|---|
| 1 ————————— | 2 |
| 3 ————————— | 4 |
| 5 ————————— | 6 |
| 7 ————————— | 8 |
| 9 ————————— | 10 |
| 11 ————————— | 12 |
| 13 ————————— | 14 |
| 15 ————————— | 16 |
| 17 ————————— | 15 |
| 18 ————————— | 13 |
| 19 ————————— | 11 |
| 20 ————————— | 9 |
| 21 ————————— | 7 |
| 22 ————————— | 5 |
| 23 ————————— | 3 |
| 24 ————————— | 1 |
| 25 ————————— | 24 |

***Rice Stitch.*** Worked with 2 threads. Though fun to do, the intricacies of this stitch are often lost in the pattern. It should be used in small areas. Diagrams 31 and 32 used together. 2 rows across of Brick, 1 row of Rice, 3 rows across of Brick, 1 row of Rice, 5 rows across of Brick, 1 row of Rice, 4 rows across of Brick.

Diagram 32

| UP Through | DOWN Through |
|:---:|:---:|
| 1 ———————— | 2 |
| 3 ———————— | 4 |
| 5 ———————— | 6 |
| 7 ———————— | 8 |
| 6 ———————— | 8 |
| 5 ———————— | 7 |

This completes unit one.

| | |
|:---:|:---:|
| 9 ———————— | 4 |
| 1 ———————— | 10 |
| 11 ———————— | 7 |
| 12 ———————— | 13 |
| 7 ———————— | 13 |
| 11 ———————— | 12 |

This completes unit two.

| | |
|:---:|:---:|
| 14 ———————— | 3 |
| 15 ———————— | 1 |
| 16 ———————— | 17 |
| 18 ———————— | 5 |
| 17 ———————— | 5 |
| 16 ———————— | 18 |

This completes unit three.

| | |
|:---:|:---:|
| 19 ———————— | 15 |
| 20 ———————— | 14 |
| 21 ———————— | 22 |
| 23 ———————— | 16 |
| 22 ———————— | 16 |
| 21 ———————— | 23 |

This completes unit four.

| | |
|:---:|:---:|
| 24 ———————— | 1 |
| 14 ———————— | 9 |
| 25 ———————— | 18 |
| 26 ———————— | 11 |
| 18 ———————— | 11 |
| 25 ———————— | 26 |

This completes unit five.

| | |
|:---:|:---:|
| 27 ———————— | 10 |
| 9 ———————— | 28 |
| 29 ———————— | 12 |
| 30 ———————— | 31 |
| 12 ———————— | 31 |
| 29 ———————— | 30 |

This completes unit six.
32

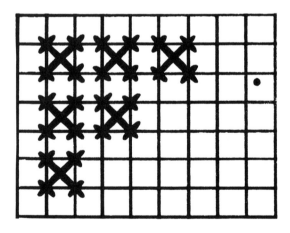

Left-Handed

***Rice Stitch.*** Worked with 2 threads. Though fun to do, the intricacies of this stitch are often lost in the pattern. It should be used in small areas. Diagrams 31 and 32 used together. 2 rows across of Brick, 1 row of Rice, 3 rows across of Brick, 1 row of Rice, 5 rows across of Brick, 1 row of Rice, 4 rows across of Brick.

Diagram 32

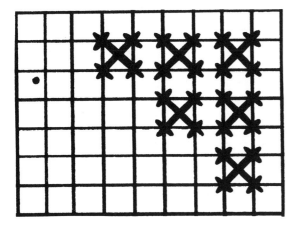

Right-Handed

| UP Through | DOWN Through |
|---|---|
| 1 ——————— | 2 |
| 3 ——————— | 4 |
| 5 ——————— | 6 |
| 7 ——————— | 8 |
| 6 ——————— | 8 |
| 5 ——————— | 7 |

This completes unit one.

| | |
|---|---|
| 9 ——————— | 4 |
| 1 ——————— | 10 |
| 11 ——————— | 7 |
| 12 ——————— | 13 |
| 7 ——————— | 13 |
| 11 ——————— | 12 |

This completes unit two.

| | |
|---|---|
| 14 ——————— | 3 |
| 15 ——————— | 1 |
| 16 ——————— | 17 |
| 18 ——————— | 5 |
| 17 ——————— | 5 |
| 16 ——————— | 18 |

This completes unit three.

| | |
|---|---|
| 19 ——————— | 15 |
| 20 ——————— | 14 |
| 21 ——————— | 22 |
| 23 ——————— | 16 |
| 22 ——————— | 16 |
| 21 ——————— | 23 |

This completes unit four.

| | |
|---|---|
| 24 ——————— | 1 |
| 14 ——————— | 9 |
| 25 ——————— | 18 |
| 26 ——————— | 11 |
| 18 ——————— | 11 |
| 25 ——————— | 26 |

This completes unit five.

| | |
|---|---|
| 27 ——————— | 10 |
| 9 ——————— | 28 |
| 29 ——————— | 12 |
| 30 ——————— | 31 |
| 12 ——————— | 31 |
| 29 ——————— | 30 |

This completes unit six.
32

***Fern Stitch.*** Worked with 2 threads. 4 units across. This stitch does resemble a fern. It can be done in a solid color as shown here, or each row can alternate.

Diagram 33

| UP Through | | DOWN Through |
|---|---|---|
| 1 | ———— | 2 |
| 3 | ———— | 4 |
| 5 | ———— | 6 |
| 7 | ———— | 8 |
| 9 | ———— | 10 |
| 11 | ———— | 12 |
| 13 | ———— | 14 |
| 15 | ———— | 16 |
| 17 | ———— | 18 |
| 19 | ———— | 20 |
| 21 | ———— | 22 |
| 23 | ———— | 24 |
| 25 | ———— | 26 |
| 27 | ———— | 28 |
| 29 | ———— | 30 |
| 31 | ———— | 32 |
| 30 | ———— | 33 |
| 31 | ———— | 34 |
| 35 | ———— | 36 |
| 37 | ———— | 38 |
| 39 | ———— | 40 |
| 41 | ———— | 5 |
| 42 | ———— | 43 |
| 44 | ———— | 9 |
| 45 | ———— | 46 |
| 47 | ———— | 13 |
| 48 | ———— | 49 |
| 50 | ———— | 17 |
| 51 | ———— | 52 |
| 53 | ———— | 21 |
| 54 | ———— | 55 |
| 56 | ———— | 25 |
| 57 | ———— | 58 |
| 59 | ———— | 29 |
| 58 | ———— | 34 |
| 59 | ———— | 60 |
| 61 | ———— | 62 |
| 63 | ———— | 64 |
| 65 | ———— | 66 |
| 67 | ———— | 39 |
| 68 | | |

| | | | | | | | | | |
|---|---|---|---|---|---|---|---|---|---|
| 8 | 4 | 1 | 5 | 38 | 35 | 39 | 64 | 61 | 65 |
| 12 | 2 | 3 | 9 | 36 | 37 | 42 | 62 | 63 | 68 |
| 16 | 6 | 7 | 13 | 40 | 41 | 45 | 66 | 67 | |
| 20 | 10 | 11 | 17 | 43 | 44 | 48 | | | |
| 24 | 14 | 15 | 21 | 46 | 47 | 51 | | | |
| 28 | 18 | 19 | 25 | 49 | 50 | 54 | | | |
| 32 | 22 | 23 | 29 | 52 | 53 | 57 | | | |
| 33 | 26 | 27 | 34 | 55 | 56 | 60 | | | |
| | 30 | 31 | | 58 | 59 | | | | |

Left-Handed

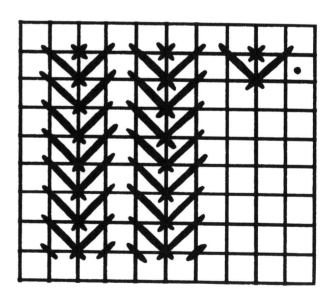

***Fern Stitch.*** Worked with 2 threads. 4 units across. This stitch does resemble a fern. It can be done in a solid color as shown here, or each row can alternate.

Diagram 33

| 65 | 61 | 64 | 39 | 35 | 38 | 5 | 1 | 4 | 8 |
|----|----|----|----|----|----|----|----|----|----|
| 68 | 63 | 62 | 42 | 37 | 36 | 9 | 3 | 2 | 12 |
|    | 67 | 66 | 45 | 41 | 40 | 13 | 7 | 6 | 16 |
|    |    |    | 48 | 44 | 43 | 17 | 11 | 10 | 20 |
|    |    |    | 51 | 47 | 46 | 21 | 15 | 14 | 24 |
|    |    |    | 54 | 50 | 49 | 25 | 19 | 18 | 28 |
|    |    |    | 57 | 53 | 52 | 29 | 23 | 22 | 32 |
|    |    |    | 60 | 56 | 55 | 34 | 27 | 26 | 33 |
|    |    |    |    | 59 | 58 |    | 31 | 30 |    |

Right-Handed

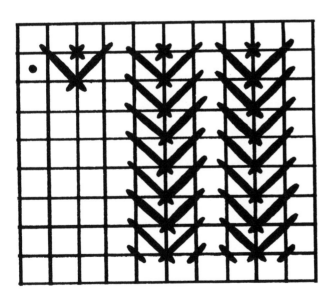

| UP Through | DOWN Through |
|-----------|--------------|
| 1 | 2 |
| 3 | 4 |
| 5 | 6 |
| 7 | 8 |
| 9 | 10 |
| 11 | 12 |
| 13 | 14 |
| 15 | 16 |
| 17 | 18 |
| 19 | 20 |
| 21 | 22 |
| 23 | 24 |
| 25 | 26 |
| 27 | 28 |
| 29 | 30 |
| 31 | 32 |
| 30 | 33 |
| 31 | 34 |
| 35 | 36 |
| 37 | 38 |
| 39 | 40 |
| 41 | 5 |
| 42 | 43 |
| 44 | 9 |
| 45 | 46 |
| 47 | 13 |
| 48 | 49 |
| 50 | 17 |
| 51 | 52 |
| 53 | 21 |
| 54 | 55 |
| 56 | 25 |
| 57 | 58 |
| 59 | 29 |
| 58 | 34 |
| 59 | 60 |
| 61 | 62 |
| 63 | 64 |
| 65 | 66 |
| 67 | 39 |
| 68 | |

Bargello and Stitchery are best described as patterns formed by counted stitches. They are never drawn or painted on a canvas. This work must be done when you can sit quietly and concentrate. There are a couple of basic rules to follow:

1. When doing a Bargello pattern, always start in the middle of your canvas and work out. This ensures the centering of your pattern.

2. When doing a Stitchery border, always do the complete border before filling in your background or Stitchery center. It is very important that the border work out perfectly.

Bargello and Stitchery are growing steadily in their popularity. There are two sound reasons for this: the first is that it is less expensive to buy a blank piece of canvas and wool by the ounce. As a matter of fact, it will cost about one third less to do a Bargello or Stitchery pillow than a handpainted design, with the yarn. The second reason for their growth are their adaptability to painted patterns. A flower can take on a lifelike quality, using different stitches. Or a fluffly animal can be made fluffy with a tufting stitch. A Bargello background can add a new dimension to a design, and a Stitchery border can be the glorious finishing touch to any piece.

There are a wide variety of books dealing with Stitchery and Bargello, instructing you, pattern by pattern, with complete stitching directions. It is essential to master a new stitch before using it. Bargello and Stitchery are tricky; they are beautiful alone, but if improperly used in a design, they can have an adverse effect. Therefore it is always wise to try out a new stitch on a separate piece of canvas to see if you are going to like it well enough to incorporate it into your needlepoint piece (see Plates 2-4).

Photograph 6. Stylized rooster done entirely in Stitchery, using eight different stitches.

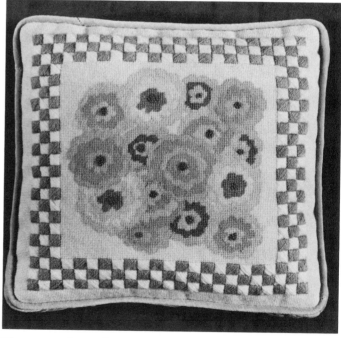

Photograph 7. Zinnia pillow done in Basketweave, accented with French Knots, and framed with a Scotch Stitch border.

Photograph 8. Square Stitchery pillow in a geometric design, using ten different stitches.

Photograph 9. Twenty-four stitches make up this patchwork sampler pillow.

Although there are many differing opinions, I feel that Stitchery and Bargello are best done on #14 canvas. When doing Stitchery on this mesh canvas, two threads of wool are sufficient, except on the Old Florentine, which goes over so many canvas threads, that a full strand of yard is needed to cover well. When doing Bargello on this size canvas, a full strand of wool must be used. Some people would prefer to use #12 canvas. If you are one of these people, then you must use a full strand of wool when doing Stitchery, as well as Bargello.

This is only a starter in Stitchery. There are well over two hundred different stitches and combinations of stitches, but these thirty should be a good beginning, (see Photographs 6-9).

# Chapter 3

# If You Can Count You Can Design

YOU WILL have to invest in a few materials, but most of them can be found in any household. The items to look for at home are: a ruler, four thumbtacks, white shelf paper, a #3 pencil, masking tape, a hard *white* eraser, and a board that you can put tacks into. There are two items that will probably have to be purchased: canvas and a black *waterproof* fineline felt tipped pen. The most essential ingredient for designing cannot be bought and unfortunately is rarely found in any household—*quiet*. You may have to lock yourself into the bathroom or a well-lit closet, enduring the discomfort, but preserving your sanity.

Having decided on the item you intend to design and sew, you can then purchase the correct quantity and size mesh canvas.

The biggest problem is finding a *waterproof* pen. Stores often claim a pen is waterproof. However, what they say is not always true and sometimes all the work is done before this is discovered. One easy way of checking before purchasing a pen is to scribble with it on a piece of paper, take a little saliva and rub your finger back and forth over the scribble. If it smudges at all, *don't* buy it. Ask for a waterproof Magic Marker, or a "Sharpie" waterproof or the new acrylic pen. One of these should be available at a store near you.

There are some basic rules and guidelines to follow regardless of what is being designed:

1. The cut size of the canvas must always be 1½″ larger all the way around the pattern. (i.e., for a 12″ x 12″ sewing area, the cut canvas must be 15″ x 15″). This does not apply to small items where 1″ all around will be sufficient. The 1½″ rule applies to the pattern as well. Always measure the widest and longest part of the pattern, then add the 1½″ to all four sides to determine what size to cut the canvas. This extra canvas is to allow adequate space when blocking the finished piece, and tacks are put all around the sewn area.

2. Always bind the edges of the canvas to prevent unraveling.

3. Cover the board with white shelf paper.

4. Place the black outlined pattern, if a shape is being used, in the middle of the board, (see Step 1). Patterns are not necessary, for rectangles, squares, or circles.

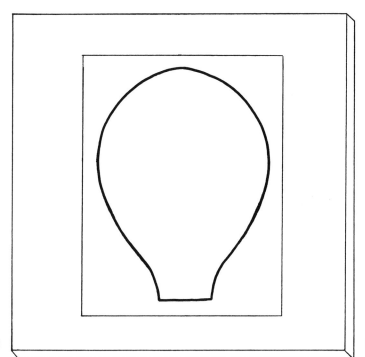

Figure 9                                                        Step 1

5. Place the canvas on top of the pattern (see Step 2).

6. Square off the canvas, tacking the four corners to the board. This is important, as the canvas threads tend to drift and draw close to the selvedged edge. This ensures your pattern being symmetrical when drawn on the canvas (see Step 3).

7. Before tracing a shape, i.e., a racket cover or slippers, check to see that the pattern outline is aligned. Use the waterproof marker to trace the outline of all shapes.

8. Use a pencil to outline squares and rectangles. Draw these lines in the valleys, not on the hills.

Each design as a specific size and shape. To facilitate your work, here is a list of patterns and their respective measurements. They are divided into two categories: Squares and Rectangles; Shapes, with a guide to the size canvas mesh to use.

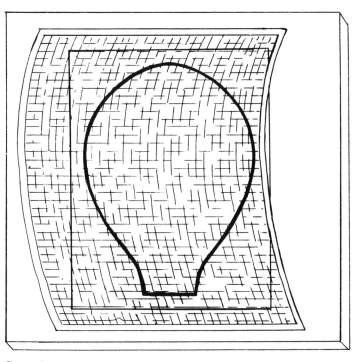

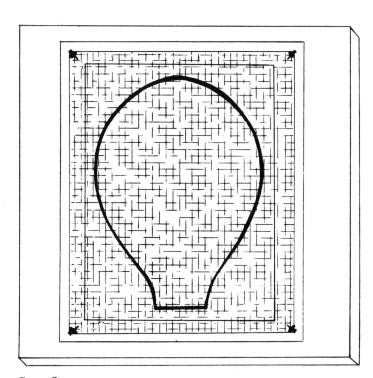

Step 2                                                        Step 3

# SQUARES AND RECTANGLES

| ITEM | SEWING SIZE | CUTTING SIZE | SUGGESTED MESH SIZE (In order of preference) |
|---|---|---|---|
| COASTERS | 3½″ x 3½″ | 6″ x 6″ | #18, 16, 14 |
| POCKET PATCHES | 3½″ x 4½″ | 6″ x 7″ | #18, 16, 14 |
| BOW TIE | | | |
| 1 piece | 1½″ x 5½″ | 4″ x 8″ | #18 |
| 1 piece | 1½″ x ¾″ | 3½″ x 3″ | #18 |
| EYEGLASS CASES | 3½″ x 6¾″ | 9″ x 11″ (put both sides on the same piece of canvas) | #18, 16, 14 |
| ADDRESS BOOK | 6″ x 9″ | 8″ x 11″ | #14, 12 |
| CHECKBOOK COVER fold over | 8″ x 8″ | 11″ x 11″ | #18, 16, 14 |
| MAN'S BELT | 1½″ x waist size | 3½″ x waist size plus 1½″ at each end | #18, 16, 14 |
| WOMAN'S BELT | 2″ x hip or waist size | 4″ x hip or waist size plus 1½″ at each end | #18, 16, 14 |
| LUGGAGE STRAPS 3 pieces | 2½″ x 21″ | 6″ x 24″ | #14, 12 |
| TELEPHONE BOOKS | 10″ x 12″ | 13″ x 15″ | #14, 12 |
| BELL PULLS | 6½″ x 60″ | 9½″ x 63″ | #14, 12 |
| DIRECTORS' CHAIRS wood | | | |
| 1 piece (back) | 7″ x 44″ | 10″ x 47″ | #10 |
| 1 piece (seat) | 16½″ x 18½″ | 20″ x 22″ | #10 |
| chrome | | | |
| 1 piece (back) | 8″ x 41″ | 11″ x 44″ | #10 |
| 1 piece (seat) | 15″ x 24″ | 18″ x 27″ | #10 |
| child's | | | |
| 1 piece (back) | 5″ x 35½″ | 8″ x 38½″ | #10, 12, 14 |
| 1 piece (seat) | 12½″ x 14½″ | 15½″ x 17½″ | #10, 12, 14 |
| PILLOWS or PICTURES | 10″ x 10″ | 13″ x 13″ | #14, 12, 10 |
| | 12″ x 12″ | 15″ x 15″ | #14, 12, 10 |
| | 14″ x 14″ | 17″ x 17″ | #14, 12, 10 |
| | 10″ x 12″ | 13″ x 15″ | #14, 12, 10 |
| | 12″ x 14″ | 15″ x 17″ | #14, 12, 10 |
| | 14″ x 16″ | 17″ x 19″ | #14, 12, 10 |
| | etc. | etc. | |
| TOTE BAGS * 3 pieces | | | |
| 2 pieces (sides) | 10″ x 12″ | 13″ x 15″ | #14, 12, 10 |
| 1 piece (gusset) | 2½″ x 32″ | 5″ x 35″ | #14, 12, 10 |
| 2 pieces (sides) | 12″ x 12″ | 15″ x 15″ | #14, 12, 10 |
| 1 piece (gusset) | 2½″ x 36″ | 5″ x 39″ | #14, 12, 10 |

* Whatever the size of the tote, the gusset length must equal the measurement of the two sides *plus* the bottom.

| ITEM | SEWING SIZE | CUTTING SIZE | SUGGESTED MESH SIZE (In order of preference) |
|---|---|---|---|

**RUGS**

Whatever the number and size of each square, when the outline is drawn, it *must* be *counted* perfectly across and down on *each* square to ensure that it matches, stitch for stitch, when it is sewn together. Rugs are usually executed on #10 canvas.

**PICTURE FRAMES**

| ITEM | SEWING SIZE | CUTTING SIZE | SUGGESTED MESH SIZE |
|---|---|---|---|
| 5″ x 7″ picture | 8½″ x 10½″ outside<br>3¾″ x 5¾″ inside of this<br>7½″ x 9½″<br>4½″ x 6½″ shows | 11½″ x 13½″ | #18, 16, 14 |
| 8″ x 10″ picture | 12″ x 14″ outside<br>6¾″ x 8¾″ inside of this<br>11″ x 13″<br>7½″ x 9½″ shows | 15″ x 17″ | #18, 16, 14 |

## SHAPES

| ITEM | SEWING SIZE | CUTTING SIZE | SUGGESTED MESH SIZE |
|---|---|---|---|
| MAN'S FULL SLIPPERS<br>2 pieces | as per pattern *<br>(see Figure 10) | 13″ x 16½″ | #18, 16, 14 |
| MAN'S SCUFFS<br>2 pieces | as per pattern<br>(see Figure 11) | 12″ x 12″ | #18, 16, 14 |
| WOMAN'S SCUFFS<br>2 pieces | as per pattern<br>(see Figure 12) | 10″ x 12″ | #18, 16, 14 |
| DOORSTOP | as per pattern<br>(see Figure 13) | 13″ x 20″ | #14, 12 |
| SQUASH RACKET | as per pattern<br>(see Figure 14) | 13″ x 15″ | #10, 12 |
| PADDLE TENNIS RACKET | as per pattern<br>(see Figure 15) | 13″ x 16″ | #10, 12 |
| STEEL TENNIS RACKET | as per pattern<br>(see Figure 16) | 14″ x 18″ | #10, 12 |
| WOOD TENNIS RACKET | as per pattern<br>(see Figure 17) | 15″ x 19″ | #10, 12 |
| CUMMERBUND | as per pattern<br>(see Figure 18) | 8½″ x 24″ | #18, 16, 14 |
| PILLOW | 12″ circle—draw around an LP record | 15″ x 15″ | #14, 12, 10 |
|  | 14″ circle, etc.—use a compass, then mark over the pencil line with the pen. Do the same with any larger circular pillows | 17″ x 17″ | #14, 12, 10 |

*NOTE: All patterns are half view. They must be traced twice and seam lines joined to create full pattern.

Figure 10

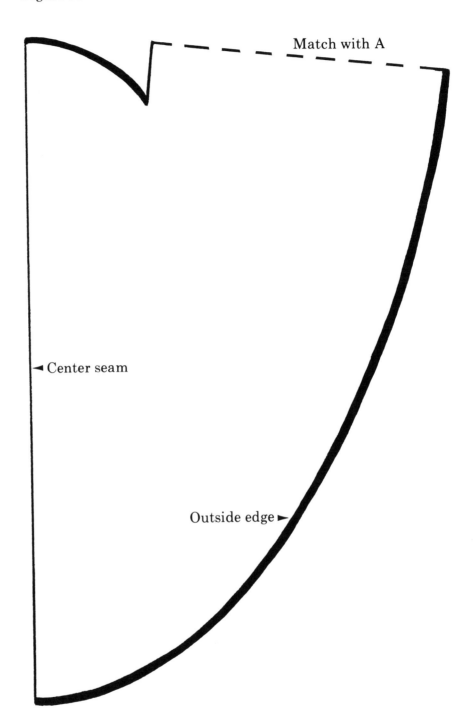

Bottom half view of man's full slipper

Figure 10

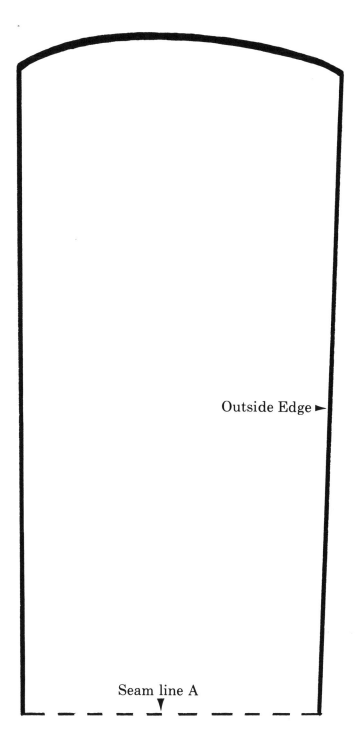

*NOTE*: All patterns are half view. They must be traced twice and seam lines joined to create full pattern.

Outside Edge ▶

Seam line A

Top half view of man's full slipper

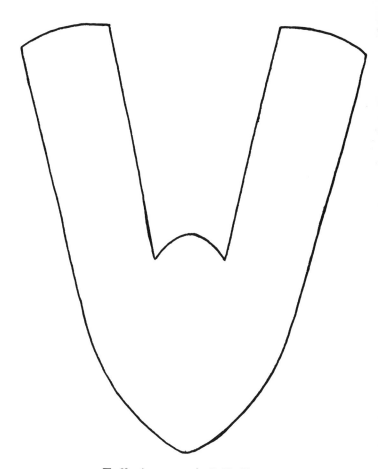

Full view man's full slipper

Figure 11

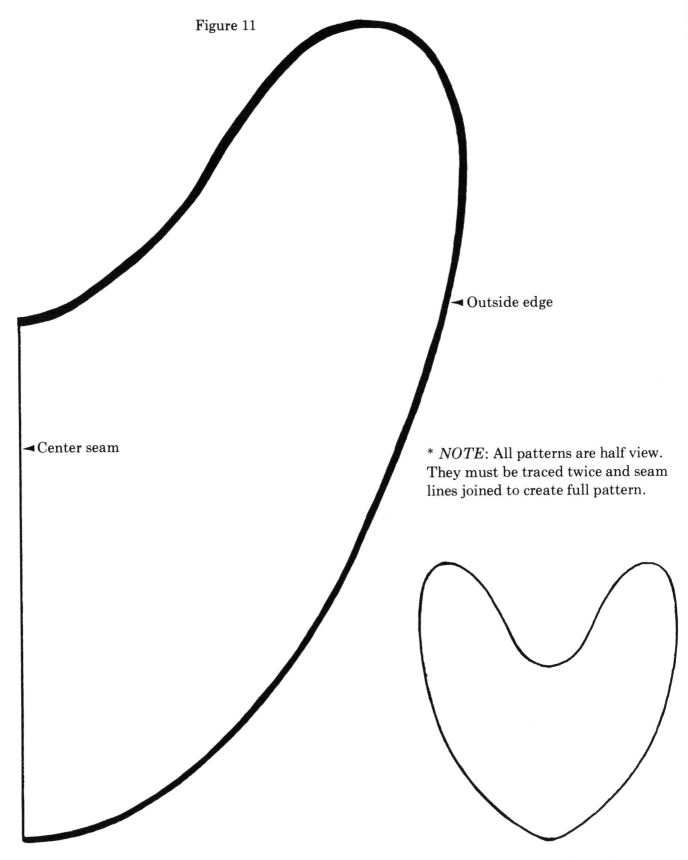

◄ Outside edge

◄ Center seam

* *NOTE*: All patterns are half view. They must be traced twice and seam lines joined to create full pattern.

Half view of man's scuff

Full view man's scuff

Figure 12

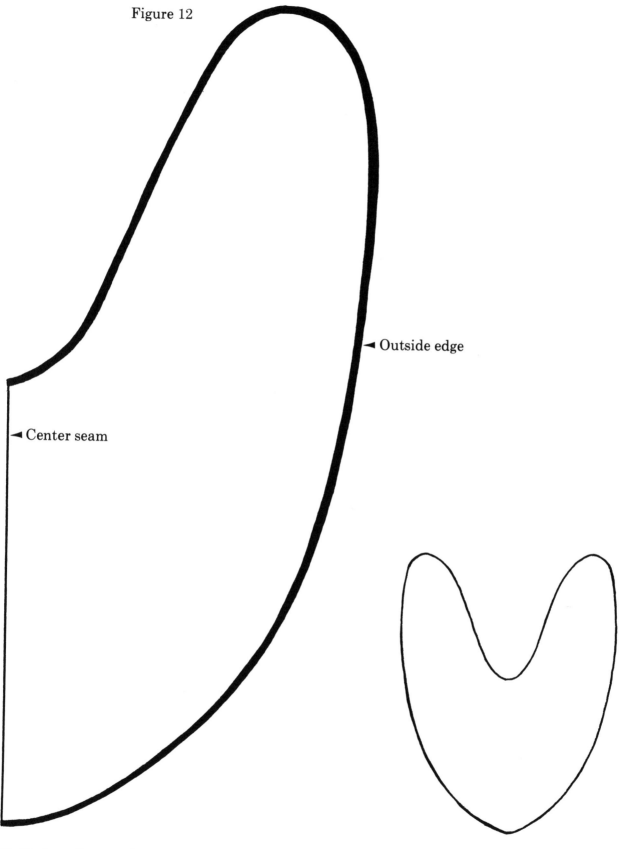

◄ Outside edge

◄ Center seam

Half view of woman's scuff

Full view woman's scuff

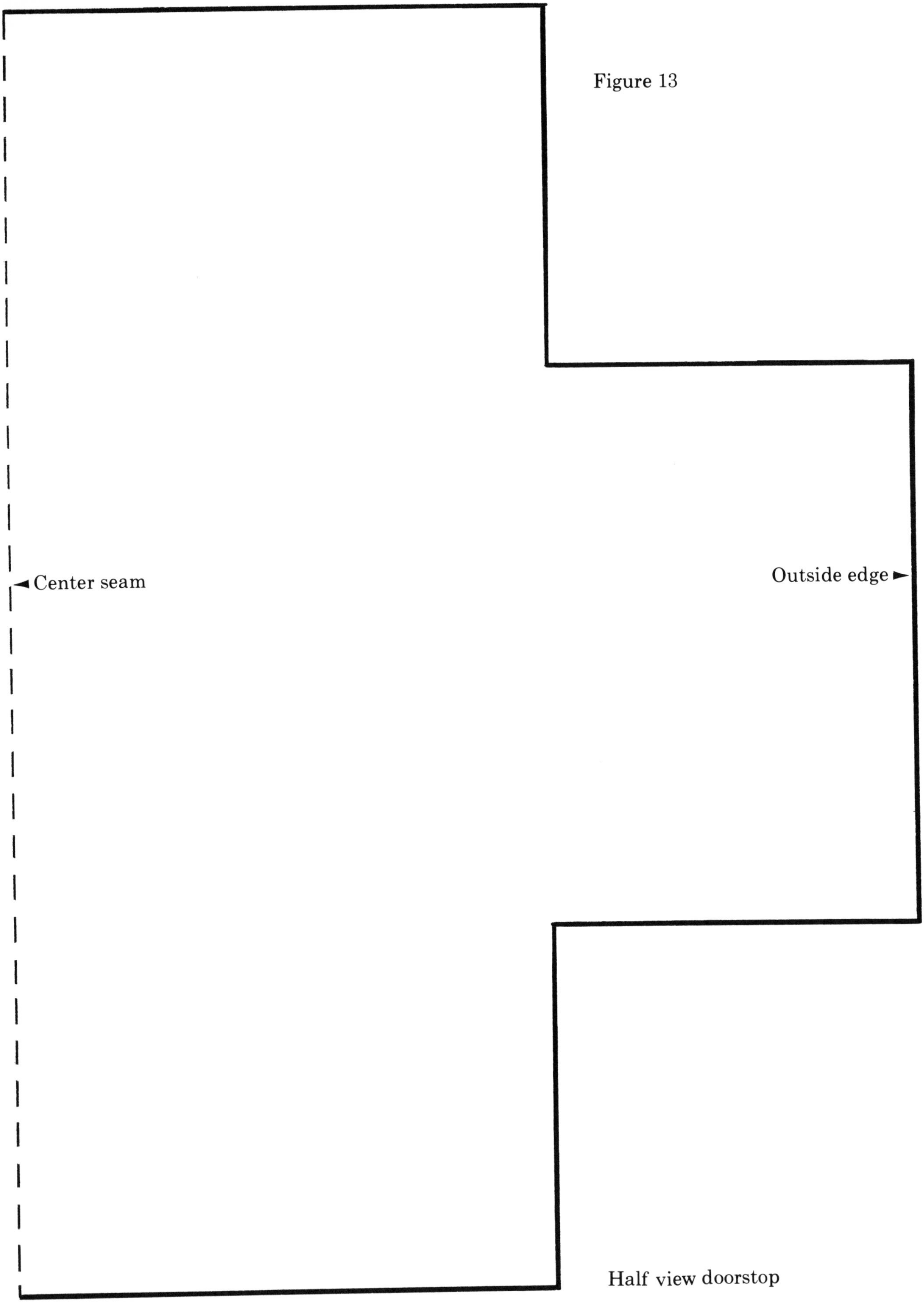

Figure 13

◄ Center seam

Outside edge ►

Half view doorstop

Figure 13

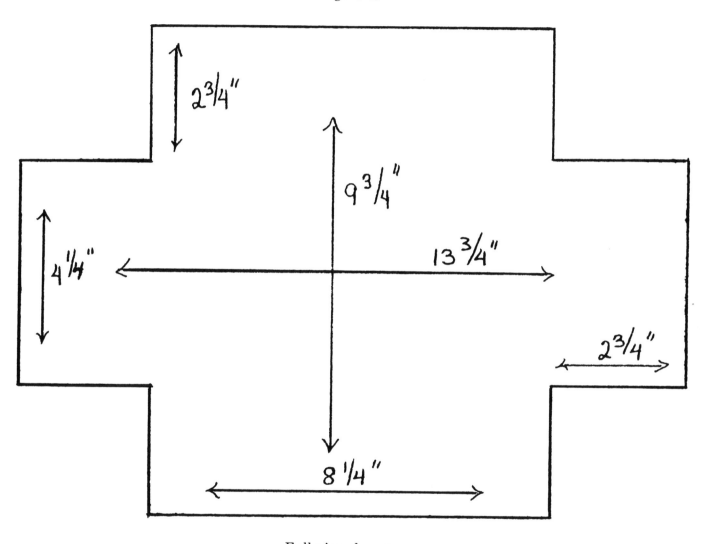

Full view doorstop

* *NOTE*: All patterns are half view. They must be traced twice and seam lines joined to create full pattern.

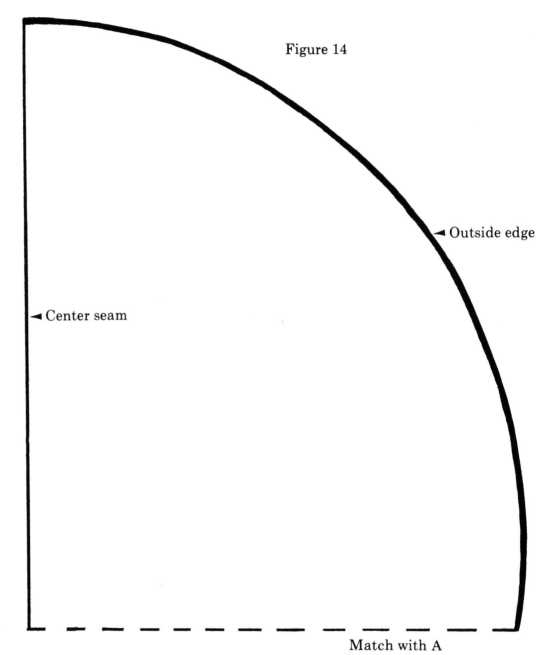

Figure 14

◄ Outside edge

◄ Center seam

Match with A

Top half of squash racket

\* *NOTE*: All patterns are half view. They must be traced twice and seam
lines joined to create full pattern.

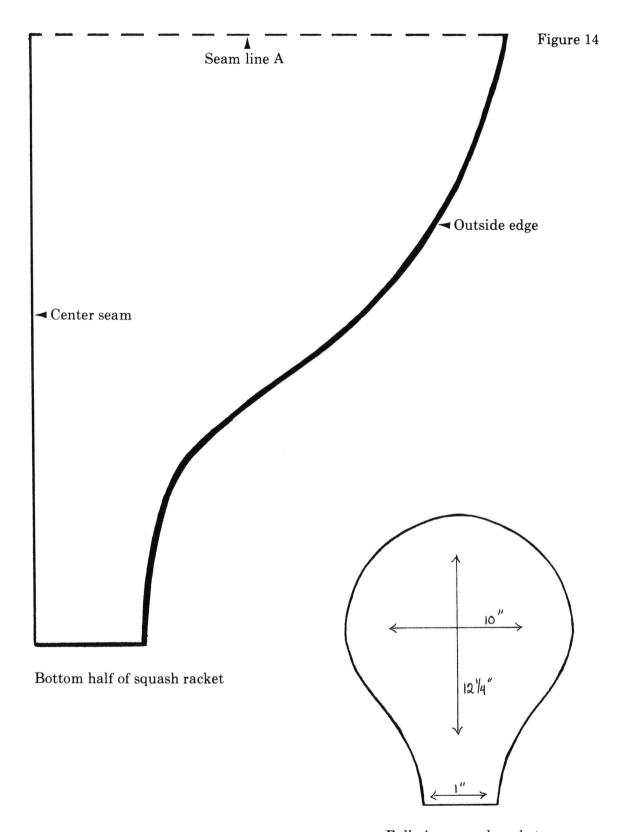

Figure 14

Seam line A

Outside edge

◄ Center seam

Bottom half of squash racket

10″

12 ¼″

1″

Full view squash racket

Figure 15

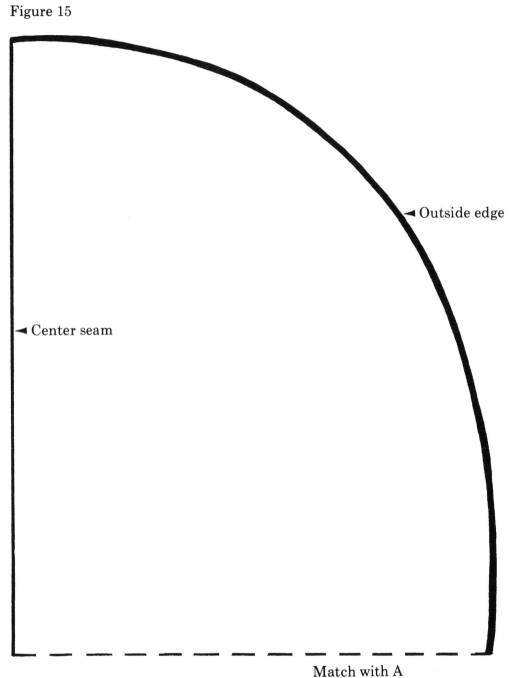

Top half of paddle racket

* *NOTE*: All patterns are half view. They must be traced twice and seam
lines joined to create full pattern.

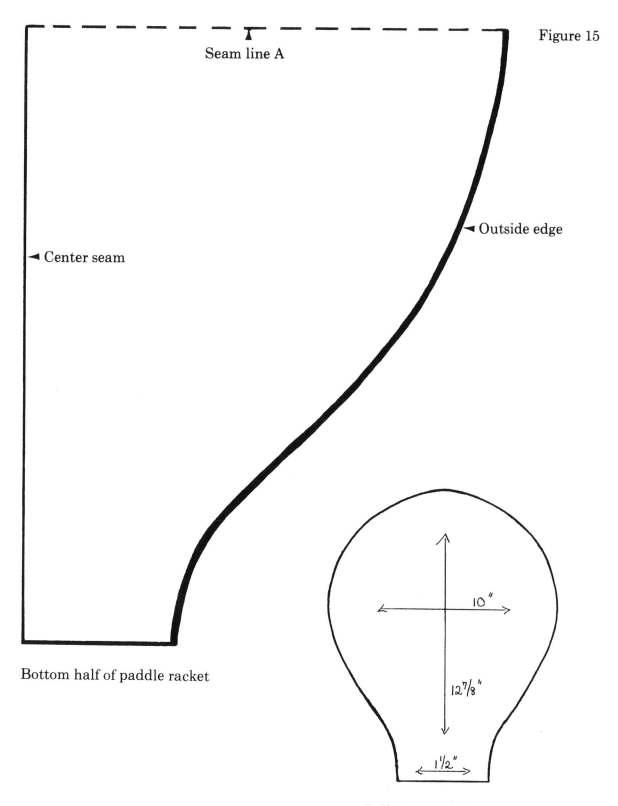

Figure 15

Seam line A

Center seam

Outside edge

Bottom half of paddle racket

10"

12⁷/₈"

1½"

Full view paddle racket

Figure 16

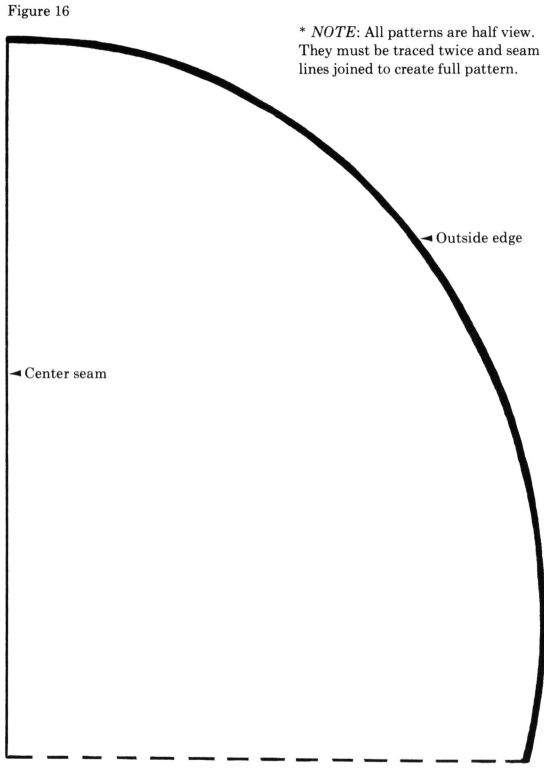

* *NOTE*: All patterns are half view. They must be traced twice and seam lines joined to create full pattern.

◄ Outside edge

◄ Center seam

Match with A

Top half of steel racket

Figure 16

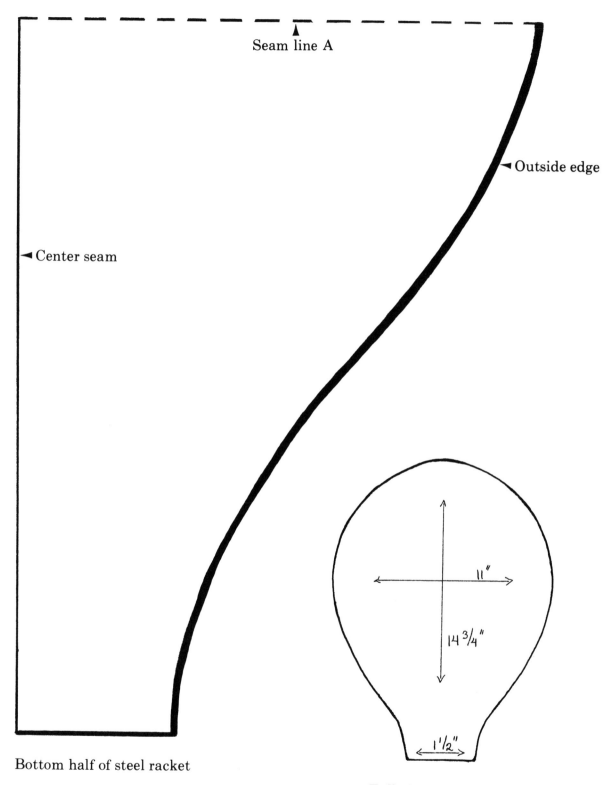

Seam line A

Outside edge

Center seam

11"

14 3/4"

1 1/2"

Bottom half of steel racket

Full view steel racket

Figure 17

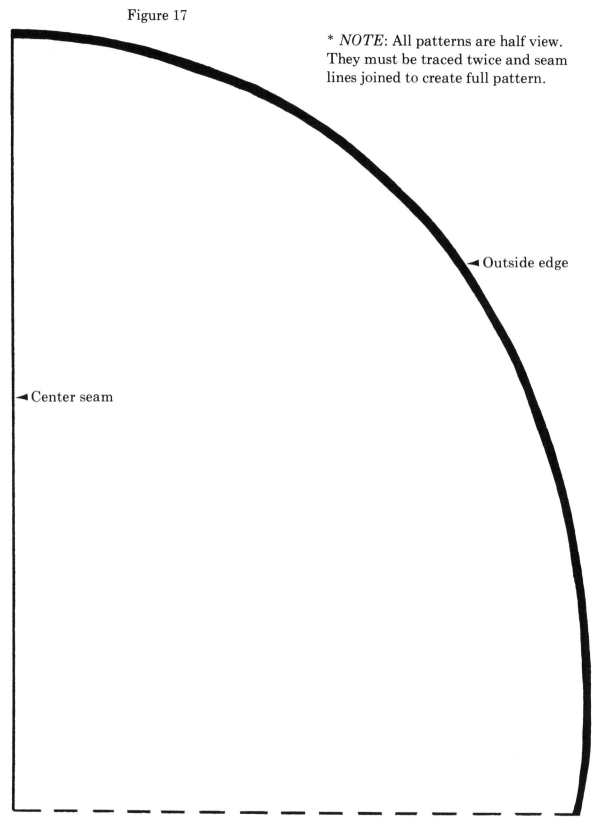

* *NOTE*: All patterns are half view. They must be traced twice and seam lines joined to create full pattern.

◄ Outside edge

◄ Center seam

Top half of wood racket

Match with A

Figure 17

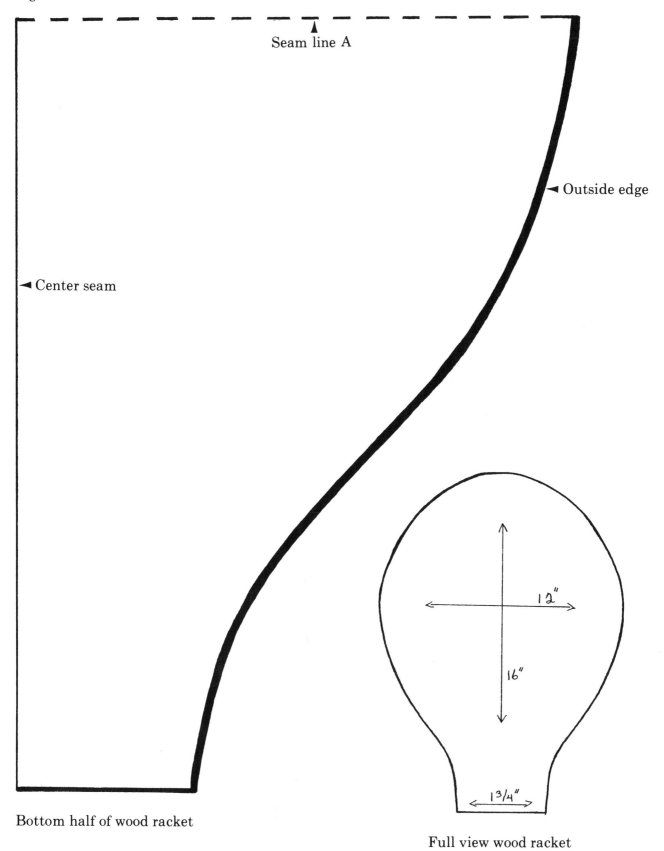

Seam line A

Outside edge

Center seam

12"

16"

1³/₄"

Bottom half of wood racket

Full view wood racket

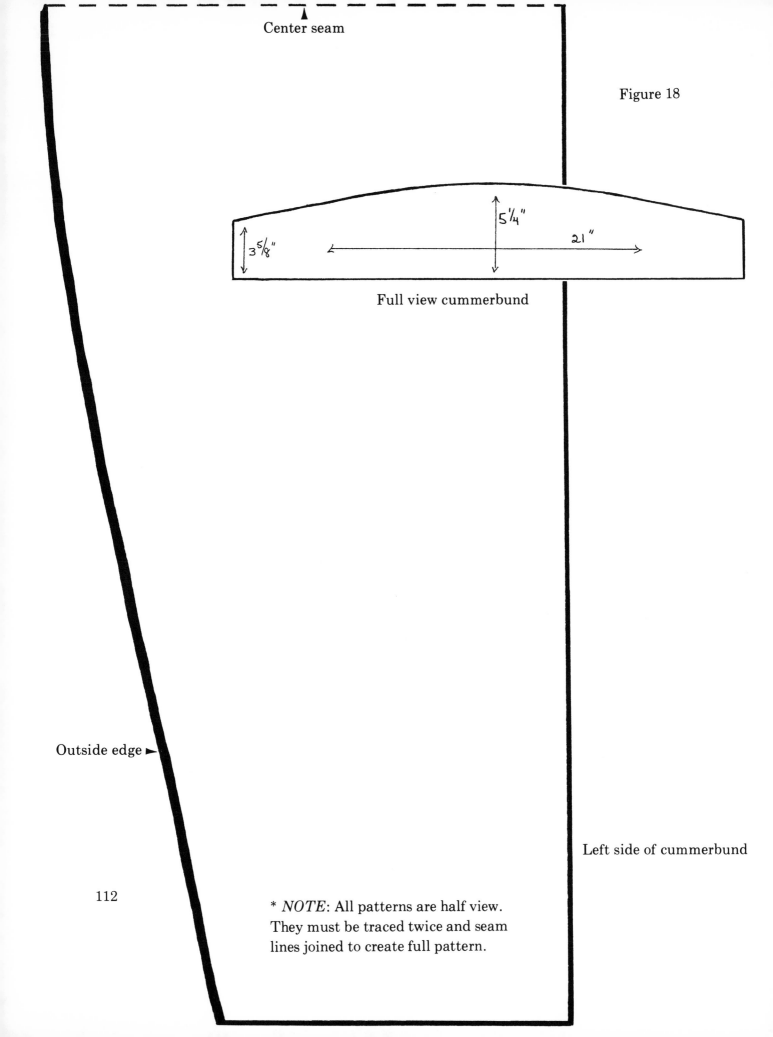

Center seam

Figure 18

5¼"

3⅝"

21"

Full view cummerbund

Outside edge ►

Left side of cummerbund

112

* *NOTE*: All patterns are half view.
They must be traced twice and seam
lines joined to create full pattern.

Stitchery is not the only thing you count—letters and initials must also be counted. They can be used as a signature on the design or as the design itself; they lend themselves to marvelous geometrics, (see Plate 5).

The same thing applies to stripes, checks, plaids and ribbons. Following are illustrations showing you how to count all these, plus examples of combinations of all these elements.

When drawing a single thread letter, draw on the hills of the canvas (see Figure 19). You will find single thread capitals are the easiest. Always draw the letters in pencil first, so that any error can be erased. When doing a set of initials, start in the middle and work out, so that your middle initial is properly centered.

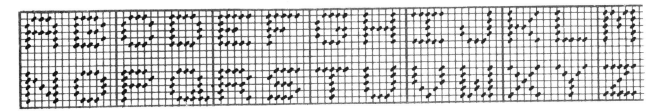

Figure 19

For a double thread letter, it is easier to draw in the valleys on the canvas (see Figure 20).

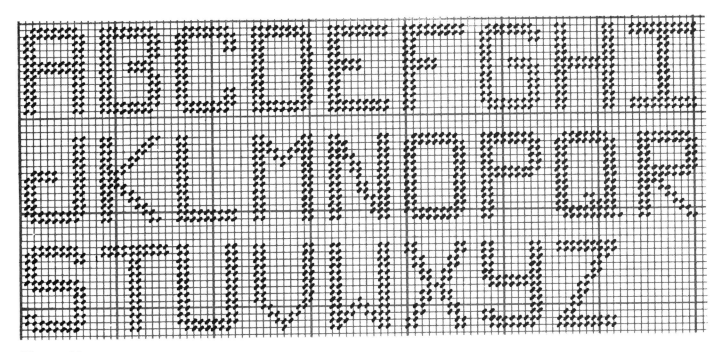

Figure 20

Three thread letters are also drawn in the valley (see Figure 21). With a three thread letter, you can use two different color wools, and get a relief effect.

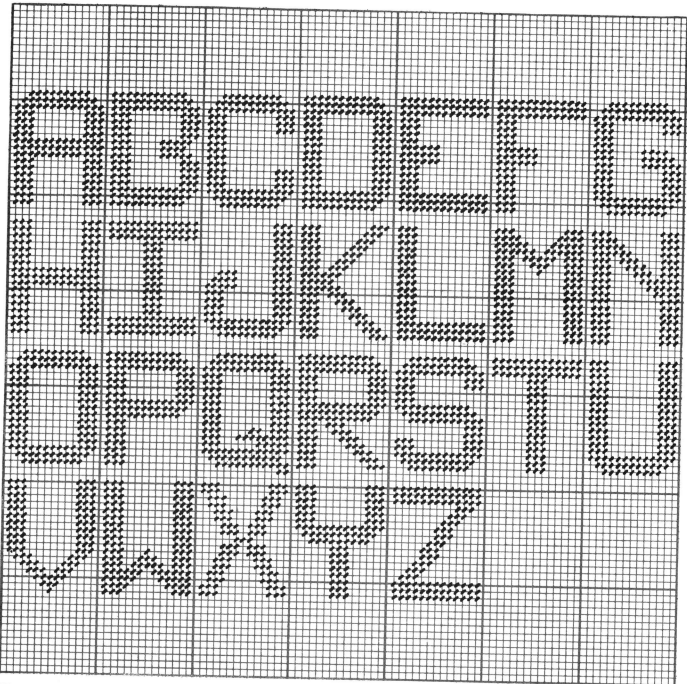

Figure 21

Stitched sayings or slogans often require a fancier letter, and it sometimes is necessary to use upper and lower case letters and numbers (see Figures 22-24 and Photograph 10).

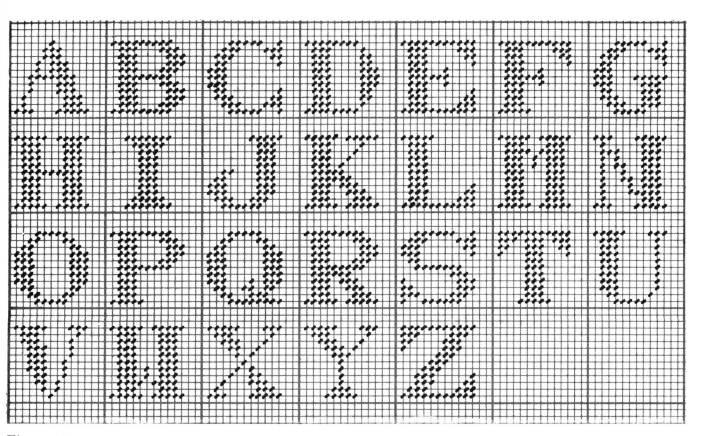

Figure 22

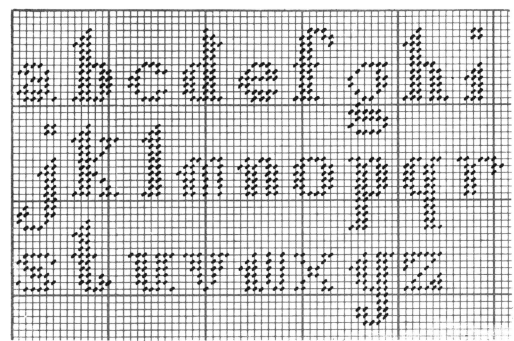

Figure 23

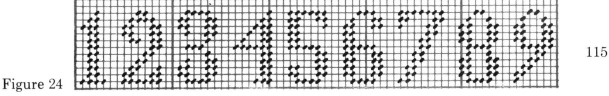

Figure 24

115

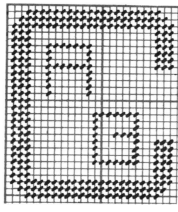

Photograph 10. This old-fashioned sampler is worked from the designs in Figures 22-24.

Monograms are fun. Here are some ideas for them (see Figures 25-28).

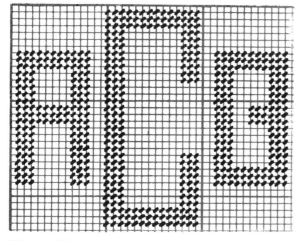

Figure 25

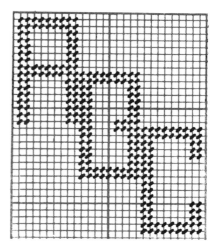

Figure 26

Figure 27

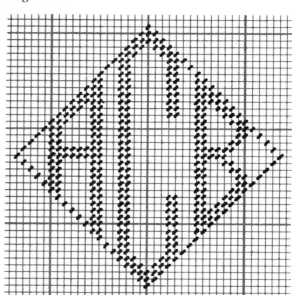

Figure 28

Stripes up and down the canvas are the easiest. They can be different widths and unevenly spaced, (see Photograph 11), but if two stripes are intended to be the same width, they must be counted. Always draw in the valleys, using a pencil.

Counting from left to right across this #14 mesh canvas, the stripes are: 4, 8, 7, 4, 8, 4, 13, 5, 2, 5, 2, 4, 7, 8, 7, 10, 3, 11, 7, 2, 11, 2, 8, 5, 11, 2, and 5 threads.

Photograph 11.

Checks have to be counted. Draw with a pencil in the valleys. Four different size checks on one piece can be enchanting, (see Photograph 12).

Counting from left to right across this #14 mesh canvas the checks are: 4 units across and 4 units down on the diagonal 4 units of 9 threads and single units of 18 threads. 1 unit across and 10 units down of 8 threads. 2 units across and 16 units down of 5 threads. 12 units across the 13 units down of 6 threads.

Directly below those squares: 36 units across and 6 units down of 2 threads.

Directly below those squares: 3 units across and 3 units down on the diagonal 9 units of 8 (equals 1 square) and 1 unit of 24.

Directly to the left: 6 units across and 28 units down of 3 threads.

Directly under the left hand corner units: 8 across and 1 unit down of 10 threads.

Directly below: 6 units across and 7 units down on the diagonal alternately, 1 unit of 12 threads, 4 units of 6 threads, 16 units of 3 threads.

Photograph 12.

Plaids can get confusing. Use a pencil drawing in the valleys, so that you can erase if you have to. The tricky part here is keeping track of which stripe goes over and which stripe goes under. Just keep saying Over, Under, Over, Under, etc., and you'll get it. Do that not only across the canvas, but also going down, (see Photograph 13).

Counting from left to right across this #14 mesh canvas the bands are: 6, 4, 17, 10, 12, 18, 9, 2, 6, 7, 23, 10, 17, 16, and 9 threads. Counting from top to bottom on the right hand side the bands are: 5, 14, 10, 4, 6, 2, 15, 11, 10, 7, 18, 18, 6, 2, 6, 6, 12, 9, and 4 threads.

Photograph 13.

Bias ribbons are more difficult. It is hard on the eyes to follow a diagonal line on the canvas, (see Photograph 14). A ruler placed along the line helps to guide you as you dot each stitch with your marker. Always dot where the warp and the weft intersect.

Counting from left to right across this #14 mesh canvas, the bias ribbons are: 33, 16, 18, 15, 10, 17, 6, 4, 25, and 13 threads.

Counting from the top to the bottom on the right hand side the bias ribbons are: 23, 12, 13, 10, 13, 4, 11, 21, 23, 10, 6, and 15 threads.

Photograph 14.

Now you can make a patchwork of stripes, checks, bias ribbon, and plaid, (see Photograph 15).

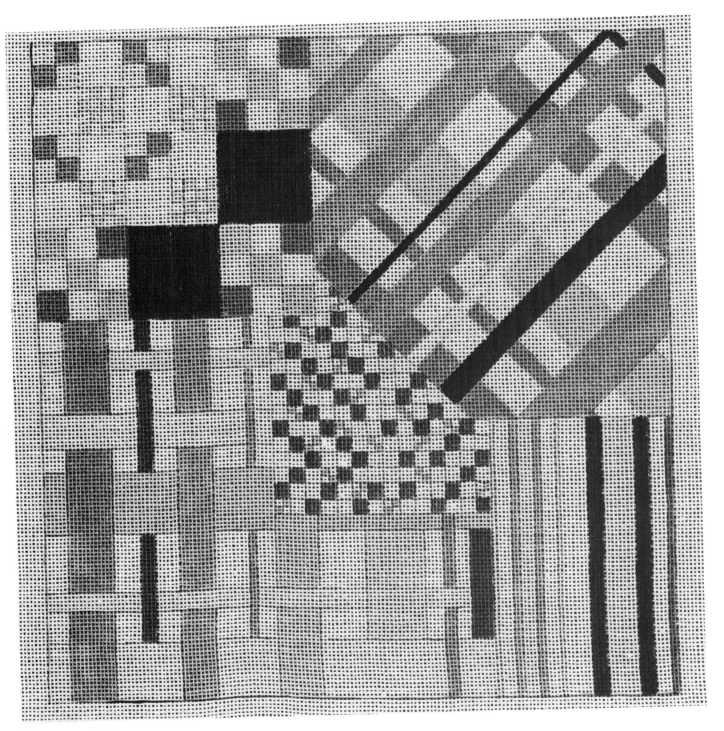

Photograph 15.

The time has come to put all these things together. Combine the stitches from Chapter 2 with these basic patterns, add some initials, and voilà—you can create a unique design! (See Photographs 16-18).

Photograph 16.

Photograph 17. One design forms three initials when positioned differently on a geometric background.

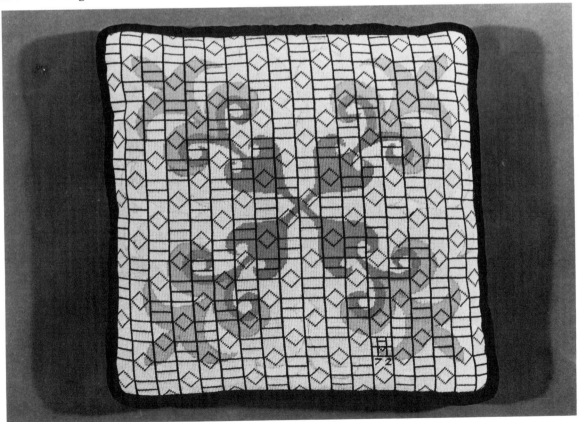

Photograph 18. The same three initials give a pattern-on-pattern effect when superimposed on another abstract design.

# Chapter 4

# Shading: Painting with Stitches

Needlepoint is basically easy to teach and to learn. Shading poses the only real stumbling block. Most shading is technique; this can be taught. But it is also an instinct, a feeling, a depth of field, and a personal ability to derive the most use and benefit from the yarn colors you are using. It is, in effect, painting with yarn. Simply grading the colors up and down is not the answer. There has to be impact and subtlety. Sometimes it takes a harsh line to make the design carry, but then there must also be the subtle, soft, touchable effect. Working in the softness of wool, together with the glossiness of DMC, will give the design a second dimension. Using DMC for delicate flowers, or an animal's eyes, nose, and whiskers, achieves this effect.

There is one easy rule to follow when shading: *always start with the darker colors first,* to delineate one area from another. This line can be exact and relatively even. The shades after that should blend into each other. To accomplish this, carry a few stitches of the color you are working with further out into the shading area. They will then intermingle with the next color. Follow this same technique until all the hues of a color have been used. I call this *flecking.* It is also effective in small areas to combine one lighter thread of a hue with one darker (this is only possible on #14 or #12 canvas) to create the feeling of tweed, otherwise known as *tweeding.* Tweeding, if properly done, can make a sensational background.

The question might arise at this point as to whether or not I actually do needlepoint, or do I just talk about it and teach it. The answer is, yes, I do do it, but rarely pieces of my own choice. Usually my spare time is spent finishing pieces for clients, repairing cut canvas, or adding whiskers and tufting to the animal designs they bring in. Every so often I get the urge to do something for the sheer joy of stitching, and it always involves shading. Two designs I created and stitched are shown in Plate 6.

***Winter Weasel.*** This was done as a study to achieve the effect of white on white. White on white is as difficult to work with as black on black. They are both hard on the eyes.

124

It is best to work them under good artificial light or north light, as bright sunlight makes it impossible to see the subtle changes. Anyone looking for a challenge in needlepoint will find it working in whites or blacks. The coldness of the blue background, combined with the snowflakes gives the aura of cold winter, and the polished chrome frame completes the illusion.

***Baby Leopard.*** The cub asleep on the bottom of my attaché case looks very young and soft. Because he is such a baby, his furry coat had to look slightly blotchy and scruffy, the way cubs really are. It isn't until they reach maturity that their coats become sleek and satiny. By putting him on a solid dark background, he looks totally alone and undisturbed.

Because of my fascination with shading, I never cease to be intrigued watching a beginner gain expertise in it.

Thanks to one of our delightful customers, Mrs. Blanche Shapiro, this progression can be shown, and delineated, (see Plate 7).

***Owls.*** In her first attempt at shading, the determination to do it correctly caused several traumas in her own household and at our store. Willing to rip out any part that we felt was incorrect, she hesitated and pondered over each and every stitch. I must admit that we all breathed a sigh of relief when the design was completed, including Mrs. Shapiro.

***Tiger Cub.*** The second piece shows the blending of the colors rather than the sharply defined lines and breaks in color that occur in the owls.

***Kittens.*** The third is a piece that fascinates me because of the sharp difference between the two kittens. The one on the right begins to show the confidence of the stitches, also an experimental urge to gain an effect with the yarns. The kitten on the left looks as if someone else had stitched it, but what has happened here is the ability of Mrs. Shapiro to make the yarns work for her to gain the greatest feeling of realism. This newfound knowledge and competence is vivid. It was the turning point from novice to expert.

***Poppy Picture Frame.*** The fourth piece is delicate and precise, an example of professional workmanship. She will tell you that she has learned so much on just this one design. Highly critical of her own work, she will chart her progress from one poppy to the next. Indeed, she is correct, the last one done does excel. However, in this case, it is really splitting hairs. This is a magnificent job, (See Plate 8).

Two winters ago I went to Africa to get away from the chaos of the needlepoint world and to see the wildlife I love so much. There were nine people on this African tour. Other than my traveling companion, I didn't know a soul. There was a couple on the airplane that I was sure belonged to our tour. When I turned around to take another look, there they sat—both doing needlepoint.

The following evening, while sitting around watching the wild elephants at sunset, they stitched, then another couple on the tour pulled out their needlepoint and they began to stitch. Here I was, thousands of miles from home and my store, and half the people with me were doing needlepoint. It was a couple of days before they found out what line of work I was in. It is to their credit, and probably one of the reasons that we became fast friends, that they did not plague me with questions on needlepoint, but continued doing their pieces quietly on their own. Out of this trip not only came lovely friendships, but also some beautiful needlepoint.

*Hippopotamus Pillow.* This was done after our trip by Mrs. Joyce Stearns. It was the first piece that she had to really shade, and it is an impressive accomplishment, (See Plate 9).

*Lion Cubs.* This pillow was also done by her following our trip last year. She will agree with me when I say there is a greater sureness and subtlety in the cubs than in the hippopotamus. It is due partially to a total understanding of her subject matter, and partially to a growing competency with the needle, (See Plate 9).

# Chapter 5

# Finishing: the Final Touch

As WITH everything in life, there are things one can or cannot do. My philosophy is to take pride in the things I can do, and putting pride aside, let others do the things I cannot. This philosophy is very applicable when it comes to needlepoint finishing. There are excellent books available on how to finish practically any item in needlepoint, all with detailed diagrams. Even following these diagrams and instructions, it is almost always painfully obvious when I have mounted something myself. I find great consolation in the fact that there are huge mounting firms that make their livelihoods out of this profession and even specialize in finishing certain select items.

Since this book is not an encyclopedia, and strongly believing that I should never teach, tell or diagram anything I cannot do myself, this chapter will only deal with the basics. If you are a do-it-yourselfer, this will certainly give you a healthy start.

It is a rarity when needlepoint does not need to be blocked. Drifting of the canvas threads even before a stitch has been taken (as discussed in Chapter 2) and the fact that stitching pulls the canvas, makes it almost compulsory.

Sometimes, on a small piece, a steam iron will do the job. If this is the case, place the canvas face down on the ironing board, pin down the bottom edge, and spread a damp clean pressing cloth over the stitched area. Press down, with the iron pulling the canvas, until the sides are at right angles to the bottom. When it is in shape, pin down the other three sides and let it cool and dry before removing it from the board.

With all the handling a canvas gets, it often becomes dirty. Needlepoint can be washed, providing the pen, paint (or markers) and yard are *colorfast*. If there is any doubt about this, *do not* submerge the piece in water. Before a canvas is washed, seam binding tape or strips of white cotton material should be sewn tightly around the edges to prevent fraying. Any sticky tape will come off in water. Woolite and cold water work beautifully. Here's how:

1. Dunk the piece up and down, *do not* scrub or rub.

127

2. Rinse thoroughly in lots of cold water.

3. Roll the piece tightly in a terrycloth towel, *do not* wring out, soaking up most of the water.

4. Roll the piece up in a second towel to remove all excess water.

5. Block. Blocking is essential after washing, otherwise it will dry out of shape.

Should you not be able to wash your canvas, you can clean it with K2r®. Following the instructions on the can, spray, and let dry, then vacuum or gently brush off the white powder it forms, along with the dirt. It sometimes takes three treatments, but it works amazingly well, and no harm will come to your needlepoint.

Blocking is a matter of proper equipment, patience, and muscle. Materials needed for blocking:

A board four inches bigger than the piece being blocked, one inch thick

A nice heavy hammer

A ruler or T-Square

Water

Paper toweling

Rustproof nails, one inch long, preferably with heads, to prevent hammering the fingers. (Pushpins or thumbtacks are fine provided the needlepoint is not badly out of shape and relatively small, otherwise you need the leverage that nails give).

Plate 1. *Stitchery pillow*: This was designed specifically for the purpose of learning the different stitches and to show ways of combining the same stitches to create different effects. There are twenty-seven stitches in all. The pillow measures 13½″ x 11¼″ and has been worked on #14 canvas in Persian yarn. It is designed and diagrammed for both right- and left-handed stitchers.

Plate 2. *Patchwork stitchery picture*: A multitude of stitches and colors in a personalized sampler.

Plate 3. *Toucan Pete*: Bold and colorful, it is enhanced by a variety of stitches.

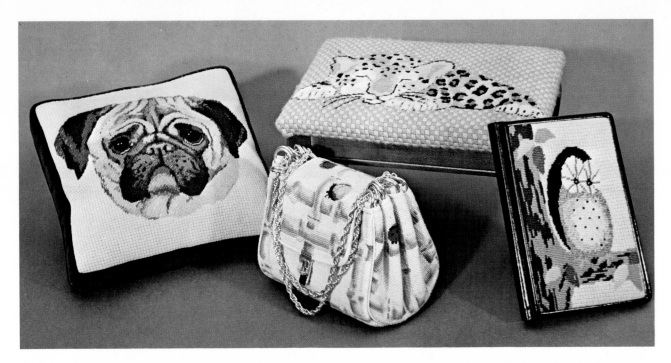

Plate 4. *Pug dog pillow*: Mosaic stitch background. *Leopard stool*: Scotch stitch on two-tone background. *Owl address book*: Mosaic stitch background. *Bamboo pocketbook*: Brick stitch background.

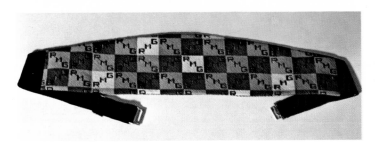

Plate 5. *Cummerbund*: Geometric and initial pattern-on-pattern design.

Plate 6. *Winter weasel*: An example of white on white. *Napping leopard cub*: Alone and undisturbed on a warm brown background.

Plate 7. *Owls*: A first attempt at shading, with effective results. *Tiger cub*: Remarkable progress on the second piece. *Kittens*: Confidence leads to experimentation on this third design. Note the difference in the kittens; the one on the left has a greater finesse than the one done first on the right.

Plate 8. *Poppy picture frame*: The fourth piece of shading—a professional achievement.

Plate 9. *Hippopotamus pillow*: An intricate and totally shaded design which was a first experiment in shading. *Lion cubs*: The second piece, it's stronger and more subtle. A handsome result.

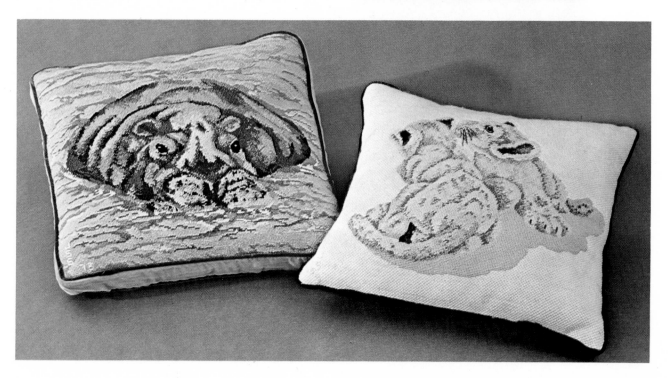

Plate 10. *Mirror; Address book; Telephone book cover; Pincushions; Coasters; Doorstop; Eyeglass cases*: A collection of beautiful gifts.

Plate 11. *Giraffe, Patchwork,* and *Giraffe-on-giraffe tennis racket covers; Tiger paddle tennis racket cover.*

1. Cover the top of the board with paper toweling, to ensure a clean surface. Turn the piece face down on the board. Dunk a wad of paper toweling or a clean sponge in the water and dab the canvas all over the *sewn* area until thoroughly damp, (see Photograph 19).

Photograph 19.

2. If the piece is badly out of shape, pull it hard in the opposite direction from the way it is pulling, (see Photograph 20).

Photograph 20.

3. Using the bottom edge as a guide, line the canvas edge up with the straight edge of the board. Nail it down, starting at the corner (left or right) and hammering the nails in the *holes* (not the threads) next to where the stitches end, about one inch apart, (see Photograph 21).

(If the canvas slants to the right then it is the left side that is nailed down next, if it slants to the left, go to work on the right side.)

Photograph 21.

4. Coax, yank, and pull the canvas out with your hammer hand until it is at a right angle to the bottom. Do this holding the canvas about half way up. Place a nail into position, holding the canvas and nail *firmly* in place, and hammer, (see Photograph 22).

Photograph 22.

5. Place another nail in between the corner and middle nails, using the same technique. Now fill in the spaces on either side of that retaining nail. Pull the top corner out as you did the middle section, so the whole side is at a right angle to the bottom, securing the canvas at one-inch intervals. Now, at the top, pull the canvas up in the middle and secure it with a nail. Repeat steps 4 and 5, checking with a ruler to be sure the canvas is stretched out evenly, (see Photograph 23).

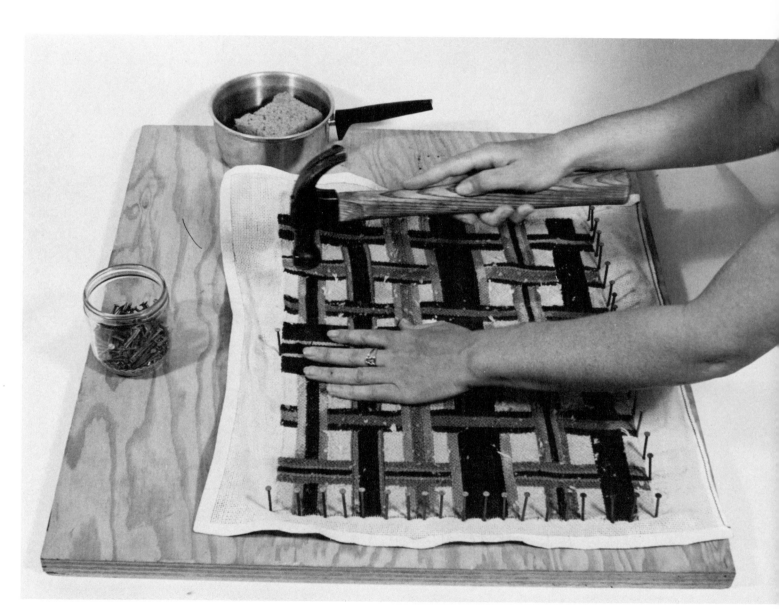

Photograph 23.

6. Repeat this entire process down the remaining side. Check this measurement too, (see Photograph 24).

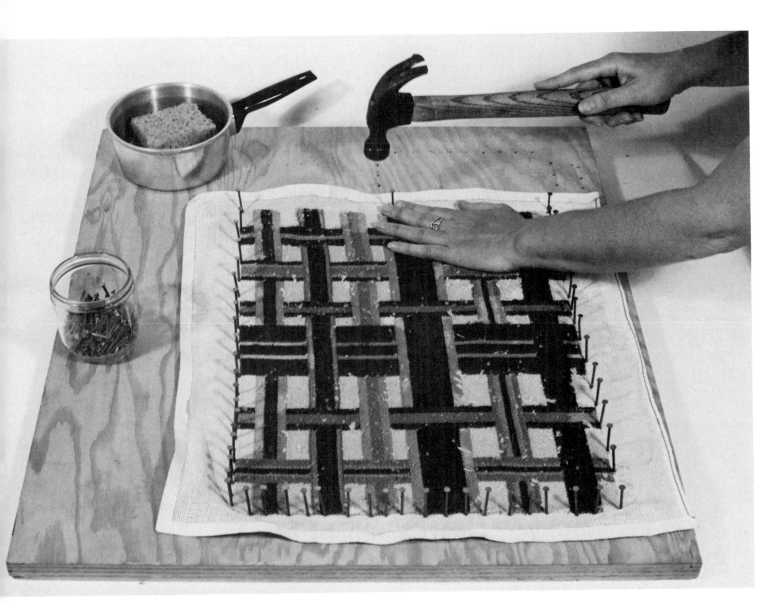

Photograph 24.

Sometimes it is necessary to pull out a few nails and adjust the canvas. It is important that the needlepoint measure the same from top to bottom all the way across the piece, and that from side to side, it is consistently the same measurement, (see Photograph 25).

Photograph 25.

Circles and shapes present problems, but they are not insurmountable. No matter what shape you have stitched, the canvas itself is a rectangle. Therefore, using half as many nails, and hammering them in one inch in from the bound edge, you can square the piece off. If it is a circle, you can lay an old record over the stitched area as a guide. Then hammer in the retaining nails around the stitched area. For shapes such as slippers or racket covers, etc., cut a paper pattern to lay on top of the stitched canvas as a guide.

It should take 36 to 48 hours for a blocked piece to completely dry out. The nails can then be removed and the design is ready for mounting.

I have often read that it is perfectly all right to block a piece several times. I disagree. Granted, sometimes it might be necessary, but the initial blocking is the one that counts. When the canvas is dampened, the sizing of the canvas dissolves into the yarn, and it works like starch. This will be lost in a second blocking, and the canvas doesn't seem to hold as well. Try to make the first blocking be the last, but don't be upset if you do have to do it again. It certainly won't destroy your canvas.

## MOUNTING

### *Footstools and slip seats*

These are the easiest to mount.
Materials needed:

A scissors

Pins

Upholstery tacks

Hammer

Masking tape

½" braiding (for footstools only)

Upholstery glue (for footstools only)

Patience.

**_Footstools:_**

Align the design on top of the stool, secure it with four pins.

Figure 29

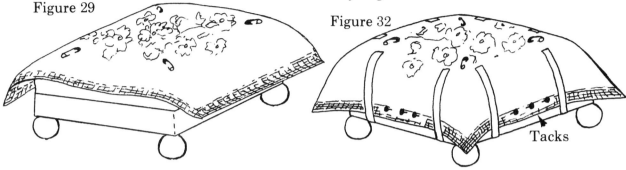

Tape down canvas in the middle of all four sides to the stool, to hold the edges of the design down.

Figure 30

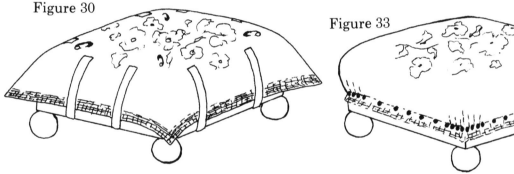

Tap in three tacks at two-inch intervals in the middle of one side, next to the stitching.

Figure 31

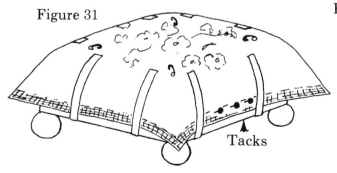

Tacks

Pull the canvas taut to the opposite side and tap in three tacks there centering them. Follow the same procedure at both ends, being sure to pull the canvas tightly as you go.

Figure 32

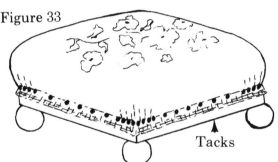

Tacks

Work your way around the stool, putting tacks in every half inch. Remove the holding tape and pins. At the corners where the canvas will have to be coaxed, put the tacks closer together.

Figure 33

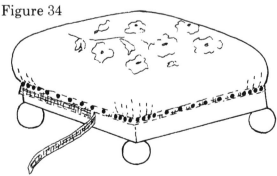

Tacks

When the design is secured completely, take a sharp pair of scissors and trim off the excess canvas to within ¼″ of the upholstery tacks.

Figure 34

Glue the braid over the tacks, pulling it gently so that it fits snugly. Use a pin to secure the ends until the glue is dry. Remove the pin and the mounting job is complete.

Place the needlepoint and seat face down on a clean flat surface and tape the four sides of the canvas to the middle of the seat.

Figure 37

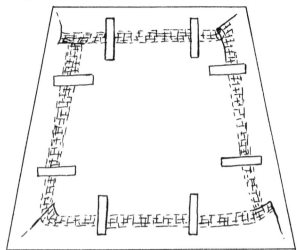

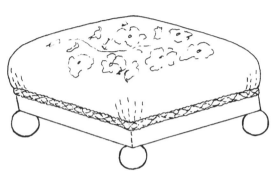

Figure 35

### *Slip seats:*

Trim the canvas to within 1″ of the sewn area all around. Center the needlepoint design on the slip seat, securing it with four or more pins.

Figure 36

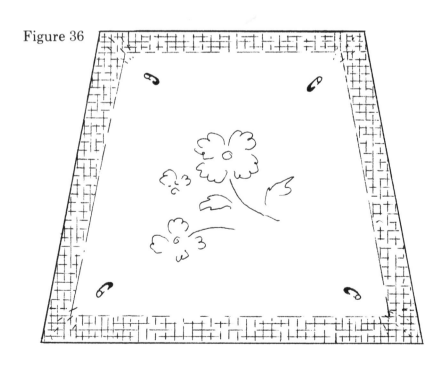

Tap in three tacks along the bottom edge at two or three inch intervals, and one row out from the stitched area.

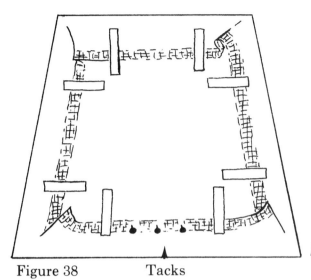

Figure 38                    Tacks

Pull the design taut from the opposite side and secure it with three tacks, as before. Then tack the other two sides.

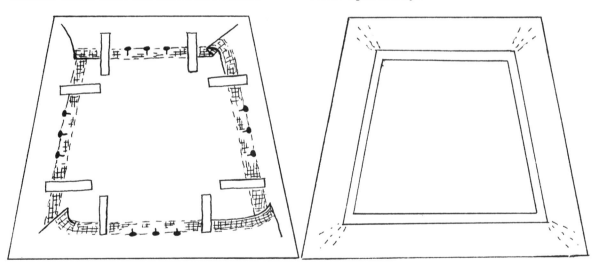

Figure 39

Remove the holding tape. Go back and tack down the canvas at one inch intervals along all four sides, being sure to keep the needlepoint tight. Then working a corner at a time, pull in tightly, coaxing the corners till they are smooth, and se-

cure with four or five tacks. Then tack the outer edges of the canvas down at three inch intervals.

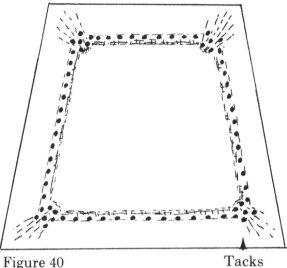

Figure 40                    Tacks

Cover the raw edges with masking tape to seal them down. Remove the holding tapes, turn the seat over, and presto, instant upholstery.

Figure 41

If you want to get fancy you can hand stitch, glue, or tack a piece of muslin across the bottom side to hide the tacks. But unless your friends spend a lot of time looking at the bottom of your chairs, it is a waste of time.

### Pictures

Materials needed:

- A frame of your choice the exact size of the stitched area or better.
- A piece of heavy cardboard, the exact size of the inside of the frame. (Two pieces will be necessary if a mat is not being used.)
- A mat board, color of your choice, the exact size as the inside of your frame, if the frame is bigger than the needlepoint design.

Scissors

Masking tape

Ruler or T-Square

Single edge razor blade

Take the blocked piece of needlepoint and trim the excess canvas to within ½″ of the sewn area with the scissors.

Figure 42

#### With a mat:

If the frame is bigger than the needle-point, measure and cut a window in the mat board ¼″ *smaller* all around than the finished sewn area. Use a single edge razor against the ruler or T-square to get a straight line, and sharp corners.

Figure 43

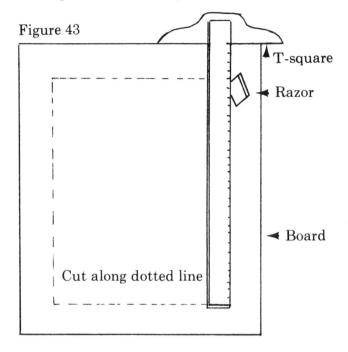

Cut along dotted line

Place the needlepoint under the mat and center the design in the window.

Figure 44

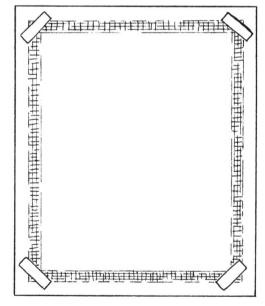

Back view of needlepoint

Carefully flip the mat and canvas, holding them tightly together, and tack the four sides down with four little pieces of tape. Check to be sure that the needlepoint is still correctly aligned, and has not slipped. Adjust it if necessary.

Figure 45

Correctly aligned

Tape all four sides down securely, sealing in the unsewn canvas edges.

Figure 46

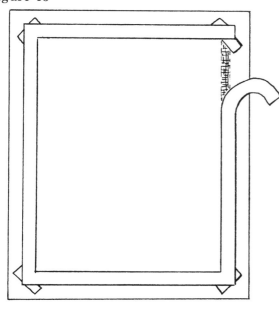

Slip the needlepoint and mat board into the frame face down on the glass, and lay the blank cardboard on top to enclose the back. Then secure the frame according to the instructions that come with it.

Figure 47

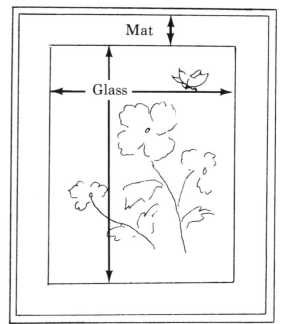

**_Without a mat:_**

Trim the excess canvas to within ¾″ of the sewn area with the scissors, place the needlepoint face down and lay one piece of cardboard on top of the sewn area.

Figure 48

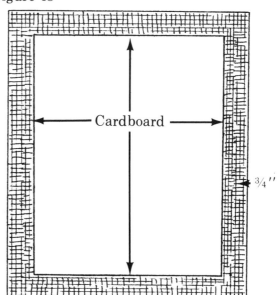

Fold the edges of the canvas over the cardboard and secure the four sides with pieces of tape.

Figure 49

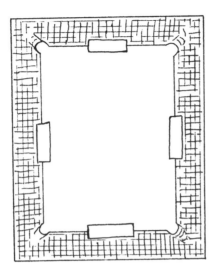

Seal down the four sides with strips of tape.

Figure 50

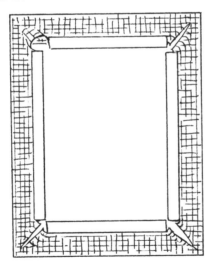

Carefully cut out each corner of excess canvas up to within three threads of the edge of the sewn area. Carefully fold in the mitered corners and seal them down with tape.

Figure 51

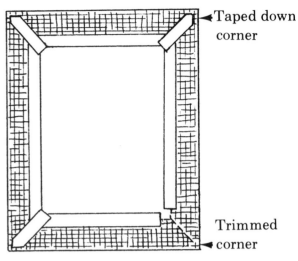

Slip the needlepoint into the frame face down on the glass. Lay the second piece of blank cardboard on top to enclose the needlepoint. Secure the frame according to the instructions that come with it.

Figure 52

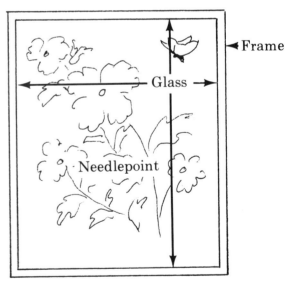

### For coasters, pocket patches, pincushions and knife edge pillows:

A closely woven heavy cotton material is perfect for mounting coasters and pocket patches. Other fabrics of your choice can be used on pincushions and knife edged pillows.

Materials needed:

A piece of material ½″ bigger all around than the finished sewn area of the needlepoint.

Straight pins . . . lots!

Scissors

Needle

Thread to match backing material

Iron

Clean press cloth

Trim the excess canvas to within four rows of the sewn area. Place the fabric face up on a clean flat surface, and lay the needlepoint face down on the material. Match up the edges so that the canvas and the fabric are even. Trim off any extra fabric.

Figure 53

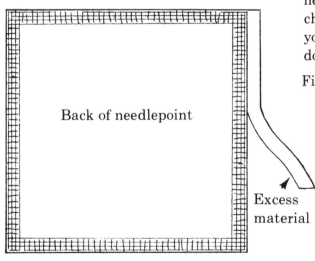

Back of needlepoint

Pin the canvas to the fabric, placing the pins every 1″ with points facing the center of the canvas. Check to see the material is lying flat against the canvas after pinning all four sides. Adjust if necessary.

Figure 54

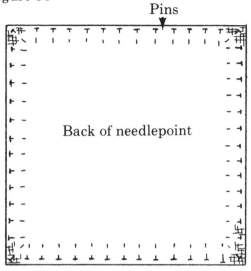

Pins

Back of needlepoint

Baste, working needlepoint side up, around *three* sides of the piece, placing the stitches one row in from the edge of the stitched area. Remove the pins from the three stitched sides. Check to see that the material is still lying flat against the needlepoint. If you have a sewing machine the next step is much easier, but if you don't, sew, using a back stitch with a double thread.

Figure 55

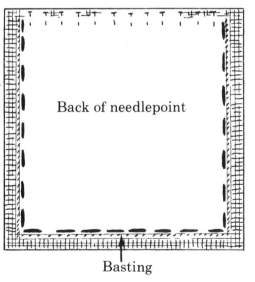

Excess material

Back of needlepoint

Basting

Restitch now with the machine or back-stitch, on the needlepoint side, this time *two* rows in from the edge of the stitched area. Remove basting stitches. Now turn the piece right side out, and press the three sewn sides flat, using a damp press cloth.

Figure 56

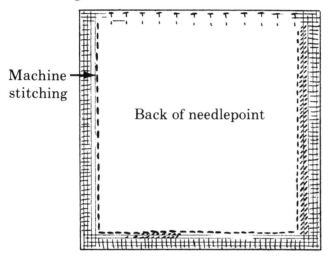

Machine stitching

Back of needlepoint

Fold in and baste down the unsewn fabric edge. Fold the open edge of the needlepoint in, folding two rows under, and baste it down.

Figure 57

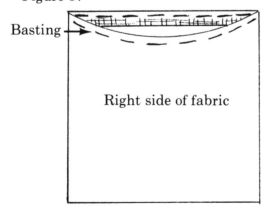

Basting

Right side of fabric

If you are mounting a pincushion or a knife edged pillow, this is the time to stuff it. Most department stores, and household supplies stores carry muslin

encased pillows, or foam rubber ones. Just be careful to purchase the right size and shape. Steel wool or stockings make good stuffings for pin cushions. Now pin the folded in edge of fabric to the folded edge of the needlepoint. Place pins every half inch points facing toward the center.

Figure 58

Blindstitch the seam closed, working on the fabric side.

Figure 59

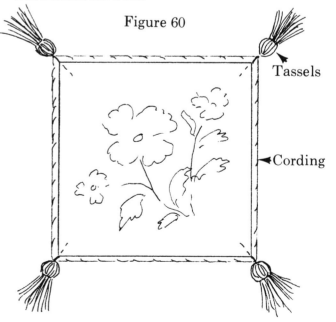

Blind stitching

Cording can be blind stitched around the edge and tassels added to give the cushion additional flair.

Figure 60

Tassels

Cording

To have your needlepoint professionally mounted, it must be taken to your local needlepoint shop. Most of the leather bound finishings are sent to one of two large mounting firms, and therefore there is a three to four week waiting period. All fabric backed pieces are done locally. There are some local upholsterers who are very competent at mounting pillows, chairs, stools, and wall hangings. If you don't have a good one in your neighborhood, then these items should also be taken to your needlepoint shop for finishing.

Although most needlepoint shops are equipped with fabric and leather color charts, they will not have a selection of offbeat materials such as checks, stripes, and prints, that can make goodlooking and different backings. It is helpful to decide in advance how you would like your needlepoint finished. A telephone call to the shop will tell you if you will have to supply your own fabric, and how much yardage, or if they have in stock what you are looking for.

Vests and slippers require a model to work from. Save yourself a trip, and bring in the model at the same time that you bring in the finished needlepoint.

Men's belts are backed with a leather of your choice, and a selection of a gold or silvered colored plain buckle. The waist measurement must be given, and, when mounted, the center hole (there are three or five) will be the waist size. The mounters allow for a change in the wearer's figure. Women's belts are mounted in either leather or fabric. They can be made to fit the waist or hip, depending on the length of the needlepoint. There are a myriad of fastenings from grommets or thongs to buckles that clasp or slip through. Be sure the width of the inside of the buckle is the same width as the needlepoint.

Telephone books vary in size from one community to another, so it is important to specify which book it is being made for. Address books and engagement books take the same size piece of needlepoint, but the inside is finished off differently, so the mounter must know what the book is going to be used for.

Racket covers—tennis, (wood or steel) squash, or paddle—must also be specified, to save the disappointment of finding out it has been mounted for the wrong style racket, and doesn't fit yours.

Picture frames are made to fit any size picture, but the mounter must be told the size of the picture and whether it is horizontal or vertical.

Doorstops luckily don't need any specifications, and you *don't* have to supply your own brick.

It is easy to see that the clearer the mounting instructions, the more accurate the job. There will be no extra delays if all the information is supplied to the mounter at the beginning of the job. Needlepoint shops are not responsible for mounting—they only handle it as a service to their clientele. Should an error be made in the mounting, they will do everything possible to see that it is corrected. However, since it is not done in their workrooms, it is difficult for them to control. By and large, there are few errors, and the needlepoint pieces come back from the mounters, beautifully finished. Professional finishing is costly, but it is due to the hand labor that goes into each and every piece, (see Plates 10 and 11). It is money well spent if, like me, you cannot do a professional job (see Sources of Supplies and Services).

If you do prefer to use a professional mounter, the following list will help you in your choice of project. It gives comparative costs for various needlepoint categories at the time of publication.

| CATEGORY | BACKING | COST |
|---|---|---|
| ADDRESS BOOK | Leather | o o |
| BELL PULLS | Material with fixtures top and bottom of your choice | o o o o |
| BELTS AND CUMMERBUNDS | Leather or fabric— fastening of your choice | o o o |
| BOXES  jewelry and stud | Leather | o o o |
| BREAKFAST TRAY | Set in tray (tray separate) | o o o |
| DIRECTOR'S CHAIRS Chrome Wood | Fabric | o o o o |
| Child | | o o o |
| COASTERS | Fabric or Leather | o |
| COCKTAIL TRAY  small and large | Set in tray (tray separate) | o |
| DOORSTOPS | Mounted over brick | o o |
| EYEGLASS CASES | Fabric with no welting | o o |
|  | With welting | o o |
| DOUBLE EYEGLASS CASE | With welting | o o o |
| FLOOR CUSHIONS | Fabric | o o o o |
| FOOTSTOOLS  large and small | Upholstered | o o |
| GAME BOARDS | Fabric, Lucite (board separate) | o o o o |
| ICE BUCKETS  Lucite    small and large | Interlined and joined    (ice bucket separate) | o |
| LAMPS  Lucite    small and large | Interlined and joined    (lamp separate) | o |
| LUGGAGE STRAPS | Fabric | o o o |
| PICTURE FRAMES | Fabric | o o o |
| PILLOWS    small and medium size | Fabric | o o o |
|    large or in suede | Fabric | o o o o |
| RUGS | Fabric | o o o o |
| SCISSOR CASES | Fabric | o o |
| SLIPPERS | Made as a shoe in leather | o o o o |
| TELEPHONE BOOKS | Leather | o o o o |
| TENNIS RACKET COVERS | Leather | o o o o |
| WASTE PAPER BASKETS | Leather joined (basket separate) | o o o o |
| Lucite | | o o |

o = under $10       o o o = $25-$40
o o = $10-$25       o o o o = $40 and over

# Part II

# THE PROJECTS

# Chapter 6

# Introduction to the Projects

YOU ARE rarely too young or too old to do needlepoint—it is not restricted to being done indoors or out, because you can carry it around with you. In fact, you can even take it with you when you're traveling. Alone, or done with others, it is fun, creative, decorative, and challenging. More than that, it is therapeutic, relaxing, productive, and fulfilling. Completed, it will be there for you to enjoy for many years, and one day will become a family heirloom, (see Plate 12).

Although it has never been promoted as a wonderful form of therapy, needlepoint has helped to fill many empty hours for hospital patients, and is used as a pleasurable and gratifying exercise to regain dexterity, or release tension, allowing patients to be productive and creative during their confinement. To a lesser degree, since it keeps both hands busy, it can help the dieter, or someone who is trying to give up smoking.

It is difficult for some people, regardless of age, to sit for any length of time with idle hands. Television programs have people riveted to their seats for several hours each day, and needlepoint can be a salvation, for how can you feel guilty about spending time in front of the television when you've been busily working away on your needlepoint? I am one of these people, and while spending long afternoons watching TV football games, have done more needlepoint than in an entire week!

Like anything else, needlepoint, too, has its drawbacks. It can become addictive, monopolizing time that should be spent otherwise. Once needlepoint begins to creep into the home, it can overtake totally, covering everything in its path—chairs, walls, floors, etc. All of this strains the monthly budget, but there is always the marvelous rationalization that it is a creative art, so why not do just one more piece?

Needlepoint is made up of decisions: What shall I make? What size should it be? What size mesh canvas shall I use? Which colors shall I pick? What design style do I want? Is it too simple, or too difficult? Can I use different stitches? Where will I put it when it's done? Should I keep it, or give it away? Can I afford it?

Of course, most of these questions you must answer for yourself. However, the decisions should be made in the order of their importance:

1. Should it be traditional, abstract, realistic, or decorative?

2. Should it be functional or simply decorative?

3. Is it for me or thee?

Once these decisions are made, the rest is relatively simple. Beginners (children or adults) must limit themselves to large mesh canvas, flat colors, and simple designs. An honest salesperson will not allow a novice to purchase a design on fine mesh canvas or one that has shading, since these present difficulties to the novice.

There are always a few clients who are determined to start with a complicated piece. Short of refusing to sell them the design, there is little one can do to dissuade them. It is important to realize that your first needlepoint is a *learning* piece. The design might not be the most exciting, but at least you will not run into insurmountable difficulties with it. The mesh, though large, enables you to see where you should stick your needle. It is not supposed to be a frustrating guessing game, aimed at discouraging you from ever doing needlepoint again. Coasters and eyeglass cases always look so inviting because of their size, but since they are small, it means they are done on small mesh canvas. A modest sized pillow is the perfect starting piece. It is designed to build *competence* and *confidence*. From this piece, it is easy to progress to smaller mesh canvas, uncomplicated shading, and more intricate patterns. Circles and shapes no longer seem impossible and there is the secure knowledge that you can complete the piece. It is only a matter of time before you will be ready to handle complicated shading and intricate motifs.

Ability is the *only* restricting factor in needlepoint, not age, or sex, or the length of time you have been needlepointing. There are only excellent, good, passable or bad *stitchers*. The most important thing about needlepoint is that you *enjoy* it. Naturally it is exciting to see a magnificently stitched piece, but the real joy is in the making, (see Plate 13).

My grandmother loved doing needlepoint. She did it for years and was tremendously enthusiastic about each new project. Her stitching was incredibly bad, however, and she used to tell me, "I know I missed a few stitches, dear, but what difference should it make to anyone—I enjoyed doing that piece!" She was incorrigible, but we all delighted in her enthusiasm. My partner Lukie and I once designed a set of dining room chairs for her with different fruit motifs on them. We carefully separated all the yarn colors for each chair. She promptly put them all into one big bag, along with some leftover knitting yarn. There she would sit, dipping into her bag for a color she particularly liked, and happily stitching in square grapes and plums. It didn't matter to her which direction the stitches took. We all marveled at the seats when they were completed. It taught me a most important lesson: that it is the *joy* of doing the work that is the most important thing.

If you like to stitch, you like to stitch. *There is absolutely no difference between male or female projects.* That is one of the nicest things about needlepoint. There are no rules about whether a design is more feminine or more masculine. The only criteria are—where will the design be going in the home, or to whom. *This* dictates subject matter, not the fact that the stitcher is male or female. Many people give needlepoint as a gift, and consequently I find women stitching designs with masculine motifs, i.e., a tennis racket cover with a bold geometric design that she will give to the man in her life, and a man stitching a floral-patterned pillow or purse for his wife. Needlepoint is usually selected on the basis of association, first with the person it will be given to, and the style and colors that most suit that person.

Breaking out projects for adults to do is difficult, because of the unlimited possibilities that needlepoint can be used for. I can only extend some helpful hints. I believe an important part of the decision on what to make are the finishing costs. If you mount your needlepoint yourself, naturally the cost is minimal, but professional mounting can be quite expensive (see Chapter 5 which includes a list of professional mounting costs).

# Chapter 7

# Projects for Mom and Dad

THE TERM "project" immediately brings to my mind a fairly large undertaking, something that involves more than one piece of needlepoint. Divided into two categories, there are *projects for the home* and *projects for gifts or self use*. Regardless of the category, when taking a project on alone, it is essential to allow adequate time for its completion. It should be done in individual units which stand on their own which, combined, become an integral part of the total project.

With thirty stitches at your fingertips, the technique of counting out patterns and letters, and the intricacies of shading, along with measurements, canvas sizes, patterns, finishing information (whether done on your own or professionally) defined, it only remains for you to decide what your project will be. Following is a list of suggested projects for you to try—I hope they will stimulate you to take off on your own.

PROJECTS FOR THE HOME

1. Series of complementary pillows for one room, (see Plate 14).

2. Combination of items united by theme and color.

   a. For the living room, study or den: Needlepoint ice bucket, cocktail tray, coasters.

   b. For the bedroom: Needlepoint waste paper basket, lamp base, luggage rack straps, throw pillow.

   c. For a baby's room: Needlepoint birth certificate, grow chart, child's chair.

Any one of these items when completed can be put to immediate use, and if the rest of the project is not finished there will still be pleasure from that part which has been done. It is so easy to get bogged down in the middle; that is why I do not recommend dining room chair seats, stair treads, and screen panels as a solo project. They are interdependent.

Putting first things first, the most important issue when beginning any project is where the necessary materials can be obtained. City dwellers have the advantage of a variety of shops in which to get their supplies, where smaller communities, due to the lack of demand, are often not equipped with a wide range of canvas in different mesh sizes, full color ranges in yarns, and designs in various sizes, shapes, and motifs. Most major needlepoint stores throughout the country have catalogs. If, in looking through these brochures there is some design that interests you, write and tell the store about your project and see if they can accommodate your needs. They are quite used to doing business by mail and should be willing to send you sketches on approval, delivery dates, and prices.

There is a growing trend toward designing needlepoint for oneself. It is certainly less costly than handpainted designs, but more expensive than the average kit. Canvas can be bought by the half yard and yarn by the ounce or the skein. It is better to find out in advance of starting a project what size canvas and type of yarn are readily available to you, as they will dictate the freedom of the design.

An artist feels at home with a pen or brush in hand, but many of the people who are designing for themselves today are not artists. They don't have to be. Patterns from wallpapers, fabrics, posters, etc., are easily transferable. Working on a flat surface, using tracing paper, any *bold* pattern can be traced. The design should be carefully traced onto the paper with black ink. It can then be transferred to the canvas in the exact manner as tracing an outline onto the canvas (see Chapter 3) with a waterproof pen. If the canvas is to be painted, acrylics are the safest and easiest to use.

Sometimes it is easy to latch onto one good motif and get a lot of mileage out of it. Here are two themes that are ideal for pillow adaptations:

## PROJECT 1

### *Example*

Wallpaper or a fabric of crossed bamboo with large and small flowers

*Pillow 1:* an exact repeat of the pattern (see Figure 61)

*Pillow 2:* crossed bamboo with *large* flowers only (see Figure 62)

*Pillow 3:* crossed bamboo with *small* flowers only (see Figure 63)

*Pillow 4:* crossed bamboo *no* flowers (see Figure 64)

*Pillow 5:* *large* flowers *no* bamboo

*Pillow 6:* *small* flowers *no* bamboo

*Pillow 7:* Bargello using some of the colors

*Pillow 8:* Stitchery using all the leftover colors

Figure 61

Figure 62

Figure 63

Figure 64

*Example*

Wallpaper or fabric with a jungle animal motif

*Pillows 1-4:* each pillow depicting a different animal (see Figures 65, 66)

*Pillows 5 and 6:* facsimiles of animal skins (i.e., zebra strips on one, leopard spots on the other)

As long as the colors vary slightly and the sizes and shapes are different, the theme will remain interesting.

## PROJECT 2 a

The ice bucket, cocktail tray and coasters are less of an undertaking than the pillows, as most of the items are small. It is important to pick a motif that is adaptable to small areas.

*Example*

Nautical flags. Any encyclopedia has prints of these. There is a flag for each letter in the alphabet.

*Ice Bucket:* a message spelled out in flags (make up your own)

*Cocktail tray:* a slogan or message spelled out as in the ice bucket

*Coasters:* initials (two or three per coaster)

As the colors in the flags are red, blue, yellow, black, and white, these motifs will fit into most rooms. They are extremely decorative, and you don't have to be nautically inclined to enjoy their look.

*Example*

Zodiac signs and symbols.

*Icebucket:* zodiac signs of the husband or wife

*Cocktail tray*: zodiac sign of the husband or wife (whichever one was not used on the icebucket)

*Coasters:* zodiac symbols of each member of the family (one per coaster)

There are many themes that can be expanded on for these items. Unlike coordinated pillows, there is a freedom of colors for these items, as they are usually used in more than one room.

## PROJECT 2 b

Wastepaper basket, lamp, luggage straps, and a pillow in a bedroom can pick up and tie in the colors in the room. Introducing a secondary theme to a room presents few problems, provided they are in keeping with the mood. Take a bedroom done in pastel colors with floral wallpaper or fabric and introduce birds or butterflies. They are both compatible.

Figure 65

Figure 66

Plate 12. *Butterfly rug*: 3′ x 5′ with colorful, realistic butterflies shown off on a quiet background.

Plate 13. *Alligator rug*: 4′ x 10′ in impressively life-like detail. This piece is near completion, but it is so superbly worked that it is difficult to tell which areas remain to be stitched.

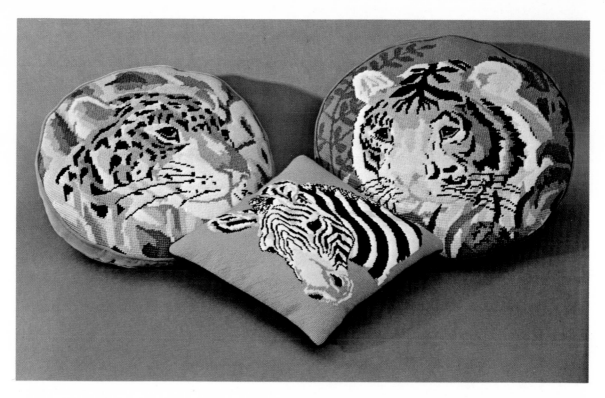

Plate 14. *Safari leopard head pillow; Safari tiger head pillow; Zebra head pillow:* As a group, or alone, they are majestic against their orange background.

Plate 15. *Leopard and cubs rug:* 5' x 7' long, this tranquil scene is framed with an intricate beetlenut border.

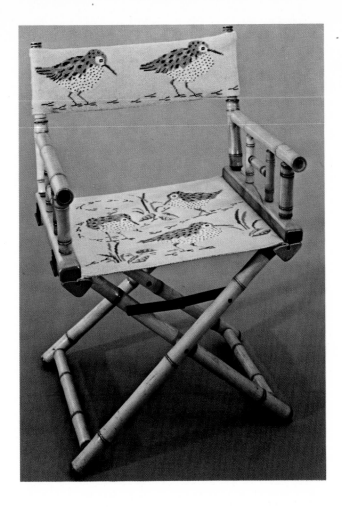

Plate 16. *Sandpiper director's chair*: Classic in its simplicity with quiet colors that would harmonize with almost any color scheme.

LEFT: Plate 17. *Patchwork child's chair*: Perfect both in size and design for a little girl.

RIGHT: Plate 18. *Noah's Ark child's chair*: An ageless theme that readily adapts itself to needlepoint.

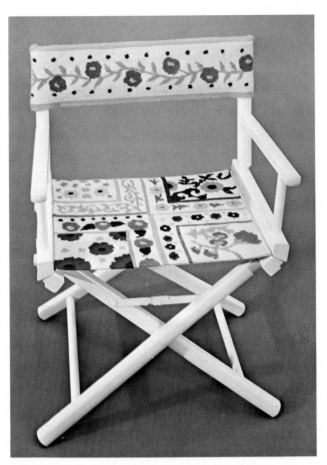

Plate 19. *Floral bolero vest*: A marvelous addition to a wardrobe. *Safari belt*: Chic over a dress or a coat.

Plate 20. *Stitchery ladderback chair*: A wide variety of stitches and colors surround a small Pooh bear. This chair was made entirely by one very talented twelve-year-old girl. She not only stitched and mounted all the needlepoint, but did all of the carpentry, painting and decorating.

Plate 21. *Christmas tree ornaments*: Packages, balls, gingerbread man, snowman and miniature stockings make very special, original tree decorations.

*Example*

Flowers and butterflies

*Wastepaper basket:* a bouquet of the flowers in the wallpaper or fabric with a butterfly hovering

*Lamp:* scattered butterflies

*Luggage straps:* flowers from the wallpaper or fabric and butterflies

*Pillow:* butterflies

The colors in the butterflies should be different from the flowers, in order to accent the theme.

*Example*

Two other favorite themes easily adaptable to any room style are strawberries and shells (see Figures 67, 68).

*Example*

Room decorated in solid bold colors where the colors set the mood. Any motif can be introduced or to keep the room simple. Stitchery patchworks that unite all the colors could be the most attractive addition.

PROJECT 2 c

Ideas for children's rooms are the simplest of all, for there are a myriad of storybooks with bold drawings to work from.

*Example*

A favorite story such as "Winnie the Pooh," "Babar," or "Peter Rabbit"

*Birth certificate:* small studies of the story characters around the border, leaving room for the child's name, birthdate, place of birth, weight, mother's name, and father's name to be stitched in the middle

*Grow chart:* a character from the story every six inches with the child's measurements stitched in

*Child's chair:* a scene from the story

*Example*

Noah's Ark. Animals walking two by two around the border of the birth certificate and up the grow chart. The ark itself with animals in it is ideal for the chair.

*Example*

Family pets make good subjects (see Figure 69, 70).
Whatever the theme, these needlepoint pieces will always hold a strong sentimental

Figure 67

Figure 68

Figure 69

Figure 70

attachment and the childhood memories they evoke most certainly will be passed on to the next generation.

Is there a definitive line as to who would stitch these projects? A man or a woman? In most cases I feel it would, based solely on association. A woman finds herself drawn toward the idea of doing needlepoint for the bedroom or child's room, and a man gravitates toward projects for the living room, study or den. An immediate conclusion that can be drawn is that the bedroom and child's room are more feminine in decor, and the living room, study, or den are more masculine, or neutral in feeling. This is true, but I feel that there is another equally important reason for this division. Women spend more time in the bedroom and child's room, while men spend more time in the other rooms. They each like to enjoy their needlepoint endeavors, so they stitch for the rooms they inhabit most.

A home is enhanced by the beauty of needlepoint. It is rare to walk into a house or apartment these days and not see at least one piece, and it will rarely go unnoticed, (see Plate 15).

## SUGGESTIONS OF PROJECTS FOR GIFTS OR SELF USE

This area is unlimited. Belts, tennis racket covers (squash or paddle racket covers, too), Christmas stockings, address books, patches for jeans, blazers or handbags, glasses cases, golf club covers, or bigger items like, director's chairs and vests (for men), boleros (for women), and many more. The subject matter and colors will reflect the lucky person who is the beneficiery of your handwork, (see Plates 16-19).

It is relatively easy to separate male and female projects when they are stitching for themselves or someone of the same sex. For instance, a man might make himself a vest with a hunting motif or a belt with fish flies where a woman might stitch her bolero with a floral pattern and her belt with strawberries and bees. If they were to make these items for each other, the themes and colors would remain unchanged. Therefore, how could these projects be divided into male or female categories? If is only when you were making something for yourself that you pick "your colors and your motif." Then it is totally personal and a self reflection. However, I would believe that there are preferences in *items* to make. Women seem to prefer stitching clothing accessories while men like to sew items for general use.

Birthdays and special gift giving occasions have a way of sneaking up on most of us. Needlepoint takes *time*. Before plunging into a project, be sure there is enough time to complete it. Thought, time, and care are put into the stitching of a piece of needlepoint. It is not something you whip up overnight, (see Photograph 26). Therefore, the recipient of such a gift is usually someone very special.

Each design is unique, for no two people will stitch a design in exactly the same way. The cost involved is hardly comparable to the effort and time spent needlepointing.

As the variety of designs and their applications is unending, it is easy to select a gift to make: large or small, simple and chic, intricate and exotic, tailored or fancy, personal or sentimental.

Since a gift is usually a surprise, it often entails some detective work and thievery. You will need to find out the person's belt size, vest style and size, tennis racket (wood, steel, paddle, or squash), eyeglass size (half, regular, or sun), and any other measurements needed. Most of this Sherlock Combing can be done quite easily, but sometimes it is difficult to explain away a missing vest or a pair of shoes! The vest can always be at the cleaners for twenty four hours while a pattern is being made. Shoes are a little bit more difficult. It is essential that the shoe mounter be given a pair of shoes as a guide to the size and foot shape, when mounting a pair of slippers. Unfortunately, it takes about three weeks. The best excuse for missing shoes is that they are at the shoemaker, and then naturally they are lost . . . but how wonderful when, three weeks later, they are found. It is best to let your local shoemaker in on your secret, because he is the one who is going to get blamed.

When planning a needlepoint gift, be sure to allow enough time for the mounting. Most companies take from two to three weeks. If you live far away from the company doing the mounting, allow for the U.S. mail service—three weeks extra would be wise.

Coasters and eyeglass cases can be given to almost anyone. But for the man in your life, a topical belt can't be beat. It will be worn constantly and is always a conversa-

Photograph 26. Zebra-on-zebra director's chair.

tion piece. Address, telephone, or engagement book covers have a special elegance. With the wide variety of colored leathers to select from, they can be color coordinated to be used in a special room. What a perfect gift for a close relative or friend.

A wedding, travel, and family photograph album with specially designed personalized needlepoint is a treasured gift. It is so elegant that it must be left out on a table and not stashed away on a bookshelf.

Picture frames are a natural for mothers and grandmothers. What lovelier way to display photographs of their family!

Pillows, pictures, footstools, and bench covers all can be specially designed and color coordinated for the recipient.

Racket and golf club covers are marvelous gifts for sports enthusiasts.

And what about a breakfast tray or cocktail tray?

These are only a few ideas. Whether a small pincushion or a large rug, needlepoint is a gift of love, from someone who cares.

Whatever your project, the most important factor is to work on a design that appeals to you. There is nothing worse than forcing yourself to stitch a design that is boring or totally alien. Needlepoint should be pleasurable work.

# Chapter 8

# Projects for Sister and Brother

CHILDREN are more restricted in what they stitch, not because of ability but by the size of the piece and the time needed to work it. I have seen children do shaded designs that many adults would be proud to have done. They are extraordinarily exacting about their stitching once they have grasped the basics.

Six is a perfect age to start children on needlepoint. It is a herculean effort for them to thread the needle and at the beginning they will probably need a great deal of assistance. It is amazing how needlepoint develops their coordination and dexterity. They are quick to catch on to the up and down stitches like the Brick or the Gobelin. The Continental takes a little longer for them to grasp but it is important to teach them the Continental right at the beginning. Color is very important to children and they look forward to using each new strand of yard so they can change color. This in itself is an incentive to keep stitching.

Given the option, small children prefer to create their own needlepoint designs. A blank piece of canvas, some waterproof marking pens, and matching yarn colors is all they need. They are eager to stitch the same things they like to draw; food (i.e., apples), cats, dogs, houses, the sun, flowers, and people. During these early stages I feel it is very important to let them design their own work. It is easier for them to stitch their own concept of a flower rather than someone else's.

Sometimes in their excitement to get started they can't channel their thoughts toward one simple motif. To keep them from getting too complicated, it is best to give them an area 4″ x 4″ on number #10 mono mesh canvas to work in. This is a reasonable size for them to finish. Once they have decided on the subject matter, they should draw directly onto the canvas, as their first inspiration is the freest and usually the best. First they draw the outline with a waterproof black pen, then they fill in the colors with the colored waterproof markers.

Children enjoy making presents. Pincushions, little pictures, Christmas tree or-

169

naments, and bookmarks all make ideal projects for these young beginners. They can do a design or a Stitchery piece in multi-colored yarns using the Continental, Brick, and Gobelin stitches. With a little help they can stitch in an initial.

The finishing is just as important as the stitching. In Chapter 5, there are mounting instructions. With a little help, children can finish their pieces themselves.

A child's development in needlepoint is usually extremely rapid. I have learned never to underestimate their ability. They often have more tenacity than adults and, if encouraged, will even mount their needlepoint elaborately.

The chair in Plate 20, is an extraordinary accomplishment. The stitchery is meticulous, accurate and colorful. The handbuilt chair frame, painted and decorated with a "Winnie the Pooh" theme ties in with the center motif of the stitchery seat with its small Pooh bear and balloons. The needlepoint is securely attached to the seat of the chair. Though not visible, the underside of the chair is as neat and tidy as the top. All of this work—stitching, building, painting, decorating, and mounting—was done by a very talented *twelve-year-old* young lady.

There are very few children or adults who would go to such lengths on a project and have the end results show such finesse.

# Chapter 9

# Projects for the Whole Family

A GNAWING desire creeps into every needlepointer's life at one time or another, to take on a large project. There is nothing more impressive than a big rug, a set of chairs (dining room, director, or living room), stair treads, valances, a paneled screen or a Christmas tree adorned with lots of needlepoint ornaments, (see Plate 21), and stockings hanging over the fireplace for each member of the family. All are treasures to last a lifetime, which will one day become family heirlooms, (see Photograph 27).

How often do you hear the question, "Do you think I'll ever complete it?" when a particularly large project is begun. These horrendous undertakings are often completed in surprisingly short periods of time. Pieces measuring 5' x 7' up to 8' x 10' have been returned for mounting within a year of the purchase. Sets of six or more chairs are completed and in use within this same time period. One might jump to the conclusion that the stitcher had devoted every waking moment to needlepoint, but this is not the case. The busiest people take on the largest projects and complete them in the shortest period of time. Indeed, the time they set aside to needlepoint is limited, and therefore they carefully map out a plan, set goals, and apply themselves to the project in the most organized, productive fashion.

If more than one person was involved with these projects, think how quickly they would get finished. There is a certain excitement when two or more people tackle a needlepoint endeavor together. And, though not admitted, there is a strong competitive feeling that . . . I will get my part done first, and, naturally, my stitching will be better than . . . If these thoughts are kept safely under wraps, all will go well; however, once spoken, it might mean the demise of any project, and who knows what else!

Put two or more competent needlepointers in a family together, and what started off as an idea for a 6' x 8' rug might turn into a 10' x 12'. Enthusiasm is contagious and, after all, since there is more than one person stitching, why not do something just a little bit bigger and better? Instead of every other stair having a needlepoint tread,

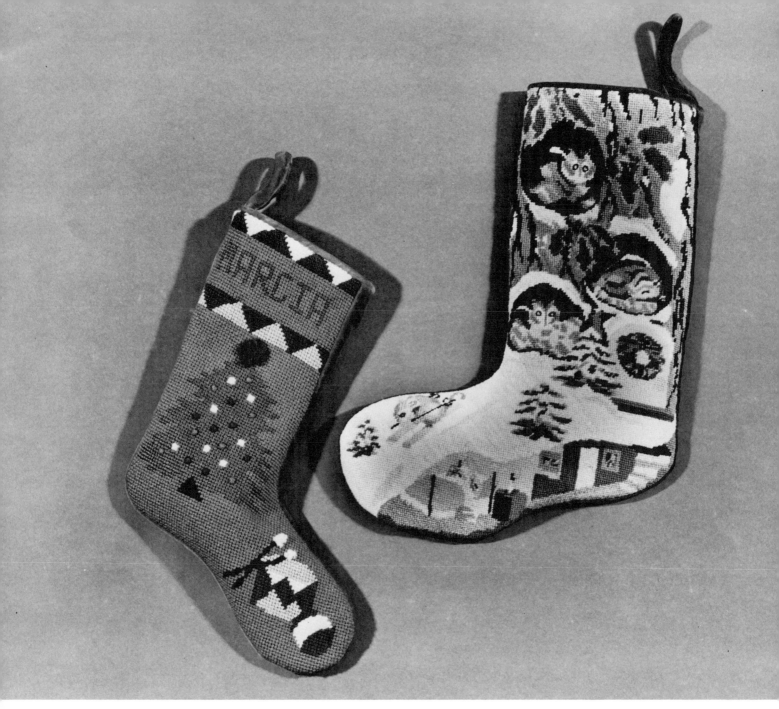

Photograph 27. Two stockings that make Christmas a little more special.

every one will. The screens will be covered front and back, and since the dining room chairs are being done, why not the two occasional chairs in the hall that go with the set?

Once settled on what is going to be stitched, a decision has to be made on pattern and color. For speed and economy there is Bargello, adaptable to dining room chairs, screens, and valances. The patterns can vary but the color scheme must remain consistent. Easily snagged, Bargello cannot withstand the wear and tear of rugs, stair treads, or loosely backed director's chairs. Easily executed, it is also advantageous in that it doesn't matter if you are left- or right-handed, since all the stitches go up and down.

There is an awful and true story I want to pass on to you as a note of caution. A couple who did superb needlepoint decided to jointly stitch a large rug. Sitting together at a large table with their work laid out on it, they each started in a corner. So engrossed were they in their work that it was not until they had worked their way into the center portion that, to their horror, they discovered their stitches were going in two different directions. Hours of work, thousands of stitches ruined because of the enthusiasm to get started. They had failed to decide in which direction the stitches were to go.

There is a very simple way to avoid such a calamity. Always mark "*top*" on each piece of canvas, and draw an arrow indicating stitch direction. This is not just a safety measure when right- and left-handers are at work, for on an overall pattern, where there is no noticeable top or bottom, it is easy to start in the wrong corner. It is a living nightmare to complete eight rug squares and find that two go in the wrong direction, or a director's chair, when the stitches on the back are opposite to the ones on the seat.

There are many themes to use for needlepoint designs, such as seasonal florals or fruits, domestic, woodland, farm or wild animals, birds and butterflies, regional or esoteric, hobbies—his, hers, theirs, and ours, travel, or adaptations of fabrics, wallpapers, or paintings.

The simplest way of putting it all together is with a workable chart. There is space left to write in items and ideas not listed. It can also become a diary of needlepoint projects done by the family.

FAMILY NEEDLEPOINT DIARY
(sample)

| Stitcher | Item | Style | Date Began | Date Finished | Size | Quantity | Design | Mesh Size | Design Colors | Background Colors |
|---|---|---|---|---|---|---|---|---|---|---|
| MARY SANDS | RUG | REALISTIC | 8/3/72 | 9/1/73 | 6' x 8' | 9 PIECES | JUNGLE ANIMALS | #10 | BUFFS, GRAYS, + BROWNS | FRENCH BLUE |
| Jim Sands | Wood Director Chair | Realistic | 9/17/72 | 2/5/73 | 7" x 44" and 16½" x 18½" | 1 Chair | Zebra | #10 | Black and white | Red |
| Lucy Sands | picture | real | Oct 2, 1972 | Nov. 15 1972 | 6" x 6" | 1 | flower and sun | #12 | red, yellow and green | purple |
| Paul Sands | Belt | Geometric | Nov. 11, 1972 | Dec 12, 1973 | 2" x 34" | 1 | Plaid | #14 | Brown, navy and orange | off white |
| | | | | | | | | | | |
| | | | | | | | | | | |
| | | | | | | | | | | |
| | | | | | | | | | | |
| | | | | | | | | | | |
| | | | | | | | | | | |
| | | | | | | | | | | |

# Illustrated Dictionary

BEFORE plunging into the world of canvas, wool, needles, thimbles and scissors, it seems wise to explain what they are used for. Needlepoint, like every other field, has its own terminology. Some of it can be found in dictionaries, but there are many other "hills" and "valleys" that have a special meaning applicable to needlepoint and therefore become part of the jargon.

*Canvas:* (As applicable to needlepoint) A strong, coarse, closely woven cloth made of cotton.

Each number represents the number of stitches taken per inch. As the penelope canvas has double threads, it can be stitched over two threads or singly, i.e., 10-20, ten stitches to the inch or twenty stitches to the inch. The smaller the number of the canvas, the bigger the canvas mesh.

*Quick point:* #5 canvas or #3 canvas.

*Gros point:* #7 canvas up through #16 canvas.

*Petit point:* #18 canvas and anything over.

*Interlock Canvas:* a double thread canvas with threads locked together to avoid splitting.

*Mono Canvas:* a single thread canvas.

*Penelope Canvas:* a double thread canvas.

*Hills:* The warp or the woof, in short, the canvas threads.

*Mesh:*
1. The open space of a canvas.

2. The fitting together and holding fast of a network of canvas threads.

175

*Warp:* Threads that run from the top to the bottom of a canvas.

*Weft:* Threads that run from side to side across the canvas.

*Woof:* Threads that weave in and out from side to side through the warp.

*Valleys:* The space between the canvas threads.

**DMC:** A strand of cotton comprised of six threads of two ply thread. Adaptable to #18 mono canvas. Easily split, it can be used on the finest of canvas. (Available at most Needlework stores, department and chain stores. Sold by the skein.)

**Error:** An incorrect stitch taken in the wrong direction in the wrong place. Damn it!

**Flecking:** As in shading, the placing of a stitch or stitches out two or more rows from where that color has been used.

**Knots:** A lump or knob in a thread formed by passing one free end through a loop and drawing it tight. A *no-no* in needlepoint, when used to secure a thread on the *back* of the canvas.

**Needles:** #13 large rug yarn needle. Used on #3 and #5 Interlock canvas with rug yarn. #18 tapestry needle used on #5 and #7 canvas with two full strands of Persian wool and #10 canvas with a full strand of Persian or tapestry yarn. #20 tapestry needle used on #12 or #14 canvas with either two threads of Persian yarn or a full strand of tapestry wool. #22 tapestry needle used on #16 and #18 canvas with one thread of Persian yarn, one strand of crewel yarn, or a full strand of DMC. #24 tapestry needle used on #16 and #18 canvas with one thread of Persian yarn, one strand of crewel yarn, or a full strand of DMC on #18 canvas. With three threads of DMC on #24 mono canvas and two threads of DMC on #28 and #32 mono canvas and 16-32 penelope (32 only) and 18-36 penelope canvas (36 only). #26 tapestry needle used on #32 mono canvas with two threads of DMC and on #18-36 penelope with two threads of DMC (36 only) and 20-40 penelope canvas one thread DMC (40 only), (see Photographs 28-40).

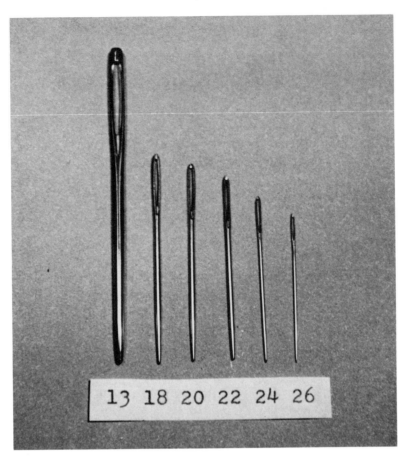

Photograph 28.

Photograph 29. #3 Interlock canvas

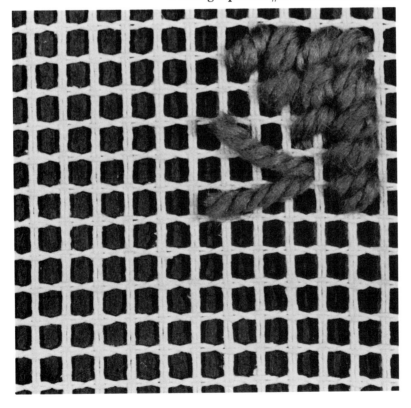

Photograph 30. #5 Interlock canvas

Photograph 31. #7 Interlock canvas

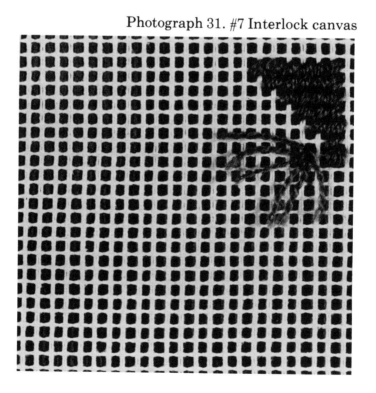

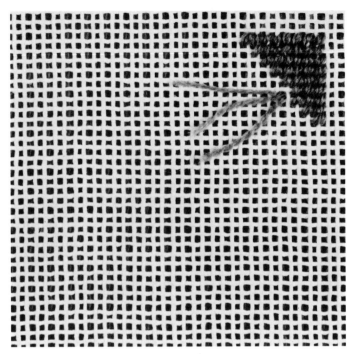

Photograph 32. #10 Mono canvas

Photograph 32 a. #10-20 Penelope canvas

Photograph 33. #12 Mono canvas

Photograph 33 a. #12-24 Penelope canvas

Photograph 34. #14 Mono canvas

Photograph 34 a. #14-28 Penelope canvas

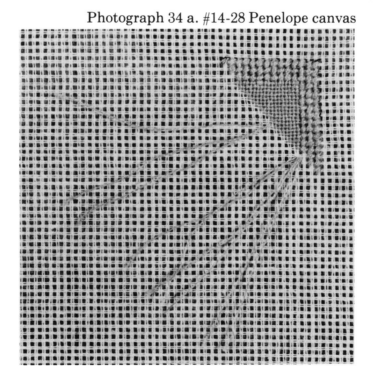

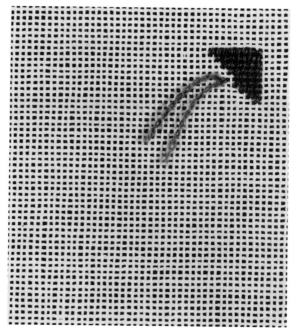

Photograph 35. #16 Mono canvas

Photograph 35 a. #16-32 Penelope canvas

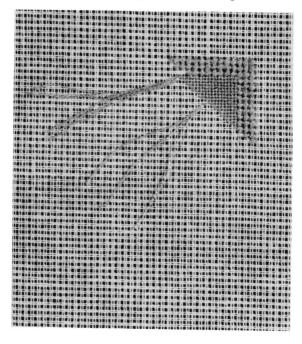

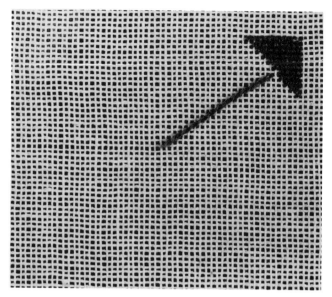

Photograph 36. #18 Mono canvas

Photograph 36 a. #18-36 Penelope canvas

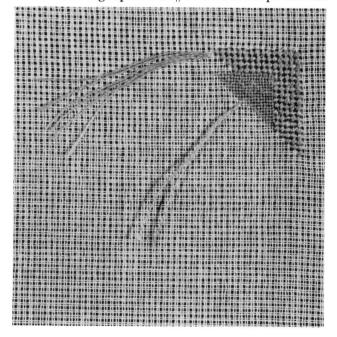

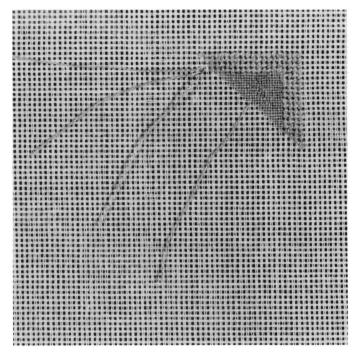

Photograph 37. #20-40 Penelope canvas

Photograph 38. #24 Mono canvas

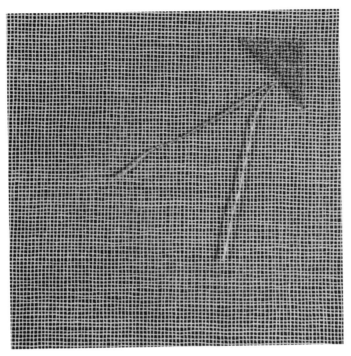

Photograph 39. #28 Mono canvas

Photograph 40. #32 Mono canvas

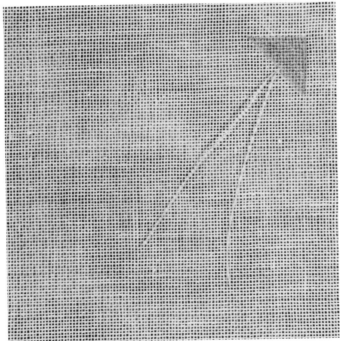

**Needlework:**
1. Work done with a needle; sewing; embroidery.
2. The work or occupation of sewing with a needle.

*Crewelwork:* A type of needlework done with crewels or worsted yarns, applied to a species of embroidery which became fashionable around 1860. Done on a closely woven fabric, only the design is executed, not the background.

*Needlepoint:* Embroidery made with colored yarns on a coarse stiff canvas cloth. Used to cover furniture, etc.

*Tapestry:* A fabric whose weft is woven, not sewn, in a picture or ornamental design, used as wall hangings, furniture covers, etc.

**Ripper:** (proper name—seam ripper) A sharp hook-like tool used for ripping, better than scissors. (Available wherever sewing materials are sold.)

**Stitch:** One complete movement of a threaded needle, forming a loop correctly around the canvas warp or woof or the warp and woof together.

**Tails:** Yarn threads left hanging from the back of a canvas that should have been woven in and snipped off, leaving the back tidy.

**Tweeding:** The combining of two different shades of the same color to create a tweedlike effect.

**Wool:** (For needlepoint) Spun in different weights for use on varying sizes of canvas.

*Crewel wool:* A strand of two ply yarn usable on #'s 18 and 16 mono canvas (Available at Needlework shops across the country).

*Persian wool:* A strand comprising three threads of two ply yarn loosely twisted together and easily separated. Adaptable to #'s 18, 16, 14, 12, and 10 mono canvas and to #'s 14, 12, 10, and 5 Interlock canvas (Available at Needlework shops across the country).

*Rug wool:* A strand of three ply yarn usable on #'s 5 and 3 Interlock canvas (Sold at Needlework shops across the country).

*Tapestry wool:* A strand of four ply yarn usable on #'s 10 and 12 mono canvas and on #'s 10-20 and 12-24 Penelope canvas (Sold by the skein in some Needlework shops, department stores and chain stores).

*Hank:* A specific length of coiled thread or yarn.

*Ply:* A strand or twist of yarn.

*Skein:* A quantity of thread or yarn wound in a coil secured by a band of paper.

*Strand:* One of threads twisted together.

*Thread:* A length of yarn.

DMC          Crewel              Persian                              Rug          Tapestry

Photograph 41.

# Sources of Supplies and Services

BOUTIQUE MARGOT
26 West 54 Street
New York, New York 10019
*French silk, embroidery thread.*

THE EMBROIDERERS' GUILD
120 East 56 Street (Suite 228)
New York, New York 10022
*A vast selection of transferable designs available.*

FREDERICK HERRSCHNER CO.
Hoover Road
Stevens Point, Wisconsin
*Kapok-filled pillow forms. Dacron batting.*

MARTHA KLEIN
(Needlepoint finishing)
3785 Broadway
New York, New York 10032
*Handbags, telephone books, luggage straps, eyeglass cases, and pillows.*

MODERN NEEDLEPOINT
MOUNTING CO.
11 West 32 Street
New York, New York 10001
*Coasters, checkbook covers, belts, picture frames, scissor cases, cigarette cases, luggage straps, bell pulls, eyeglass cases, telephone book covers, wallets, pocketbooks.*

# Recommended Books

BARGELLO

*Bargello-Florentine Canvas Work* by Elsa Williams
Van Nostrand-Reinhold Co.
    A book on basic Bargello


*Fun With Bargello* by Mira Silverstein
Charles Scribner's Sons
    A beginner's Bargello book with graphs

*Bargello Magic* by Pauline Fischer and Anabel Lasker
Holt, Rinehart and Winston, Inc.
    A Bargello book that will challenge the novices and experts.
Progressively intricate patterns.

MOUNTING AND FINISHING

*New Methods in Needlepoint* by Hope Hanley
Charles Scribner's Sons
    A comprehensive book on mounting

*Needlepoint Start to Finish* by Joan Scobey
Lancer Larchmont Books (paperback)
    Includes basic mounting techniques

## COUNTED DESIGNS

*The New World of Needlepoint* by Lisbeth Perrone
Random House, Inc.
   Good decorative stitchery patterns

*Needlepoint by Design* by Maggie Lane
Charles Scribner's Sons
   Counted pattern borders highlight this book

*More Needlepoint by Design* by Maggie Lane
Charles Scribner's Sons
   More intricate pattern borders and oriental motifs